Obviously

Obviously

stories from my timeline

Akilah Hughes

RAZORBILL

RAZORBILL

An imprint of Penguin Random House LLC, New York

First published in the United States of America by Razorbill,
an imprint of Penguin Random House LLC, 2019

Visit us online at penguinrandomhouse.com

LIBRARY OF CONGRESS CATALOGING-IN-PUBLICATION DATA
Names: Hughes, Akilah, 1989– author.
Title: Obviously : stories from my timeline / Akilah Hughes.
Description: New York : Razorbill, 2019. |
Identifiers: LCCN 2019011060 | ISBN 9781101998908 (hardback)
Subjects: LCSH: Hughes, Akilah, 1989– | YouTube (Electronic resource)—Biography. | Internet personalities—United States—Biography. Comedians—United States—Biography. | BISAC: FAMILY & RELATIONSHIPS / Life Stages / Adolescence. | FICTION / Humorous. | BIOGRAPHY & AUTOBIOGRAPHY / Women.
Classification: LCC PN1992.9236.H84 A3 2019 | DDC 792.702/8092 [B]—dc23
LC record available at https://lccn.loc.gov/2019011060

Printed in the United States of America

1 3 5 7 9 10 8 6 4 2

Design by Kelley Brady

Text set in Mercury and Gotham by Hoefler & Co

For my friend Oprah.

Yes, *that* one.

Contents

A Note

Hello, Dearest Reader.

I'm a big fan. You have no idea how long I've wanted to meet someone who thinks I'm interesting enough to spend hours, days, weeks (!!!) with, hearing exclusively about *my* life and choices, good *and* bad, and then either lending this book to a friend, buying a copy for everyone you know, or letting it sit on your shelf until one day you leave it on a stoop, opting to declutter your home by listening exclusively to audiobooks or getting a Kindle or something. I'll admit it's scary telling you everything about me and not knowing anything about you at all. If you're my fifth-grade teacher, Ms. Murphy, put this book down. Or, you know what, *don't*. I hate you and you need to read what I have to say about you and feel shitty about it. You're shitty.

If you're not my fifth-grade teacher, hi! I'm Akilah, obviously. (Or not so obviously, if you've never heard of me.) You may recognize me from HBO's *Pod Save America* series, from one of the hundreds of videos I've made on YouTube, or as the curmudgeonly lady on the G train contorting her body to fit into a middle seat. I'm old enough to remember when the internet got good and young enough to still think I know everything.

Even if you have seen me on TV or the internet, you probably don't know that I am a former spelling-bee champion, Southerner, Sundance Labs alum, and Disney cast member. I've lived a lot of lives so far (all of them black, all of them matter), and it was never really all that obvious how things would turn out. Hell, it *still* isn't very obvious how things will turn out. The world is nuts, and I hope by the time you read this book it's chilled out a little.

In the event that it hasn't, I'll be helping you find joy in therapeutic karaoke, solace in falling suddenly ill, and justice in what your acne has done to you. I wouldn't call this a self-help book, but you will feel better about your own life after reading a number of these essays. That's help, right?

My editor spent a lot of time telling me how important it is for a book to have a thread. I'm not sure if I ever found the single thread holding my whole life together, but if there is one it must be something about how I've managed to do mostly whatever I want while somehow never fitting in in any meaningful way. I saw Cher perform in Vegas by myself (fifty dollars for a ticket to see someone with such a legacy is actually appallingly low), and she did a number of captivating monologues in between songs. In one she talked about her best friend, Pauli, blowing her cover when she saw a cute guy walk into a bar. In another she said, "I never really fit in. Singers didn't think I was singer. Actors never thought I was an actor, they thought I was a singer. When I did the variety show it really fucked with everyone." And that's kind of how I feel about this book.

YouTubers never really thought of me as a YouTuber; they thought I was a comedian. Comedians and actors always think of me as a YouTuber. And my book is my variety show. You've got to stay to the end to know if it is good or not, but it will almost certainly be entertaining.

What's in a Name

My name is Akilah Saidah Kamaria Hughes. Contrary to the belief popularized by doctors and substitute teachers, all of the letters in my name are not, in fact, silent. It isn't a symbol like Prince. It's twenty-five letters, eleven syllables, and rhymes up until the last name.

It's pronounced UH-KEE-LUH SAH-EE-DUH KAH-MUH-REE-UH HUES. It is Swahili, Arabic, and Irish, respectively. Hughes is the Irish one, to be clear. Akilah means "intelligent one who reasons," which I'd say is fitting save for my penchant for overreaction to any modicum of adversity. Let's just say you don't want to be working for Spectrum if it's storming during the season finale of anything from Shondaland.

Kamaria is Arabic for "like the moon," which is both romantic and mysterious—things that I'm mostly not. Back in my chubbier years, my siblings would tell me I was like the moon in that I was "round." Saidah means "happy and fortunate," which seems like a missed naming opportunity for Zoloft and Viagra, but I digress.

Before settling on my nomenclature, Mom had a short list of potential contenders from a book on African names she still has in the house. Folasade (FULL-UH-SHAH-DAY), the HD version of ageless singer Sade's name, was my mom's first pick. My mom lived for her music in the mid-'80s, citing "Is It a Crime?" as her R & B jam of choice (I prefer "Smooth Operator"). She went with Akilah, though, because she liked the way it sounded when she said it aloud. It took her a record two weeks to name Malene, my sister, who is just a day short of a year older than me. The family just referred to her as "Abebe" (which is hilarious as it means *nothing* and is just a cool way to say "a baby") until she fired up the old paperback and decided Malene was a decent fit.

Her lucky number is six—the number of letters in my sister's full name, Malene, or Lanie for short; my brother's name, Bomani, whom we call Bo; and my full first name. And she liked what Akilah meant. Do name meanings actually affect the way your kids turn out to be? Michael means "close to God," so is that why Michael Jordan and Michael B. Jordan rule? How can that explain all the Michaels that kinda suck? Are names like astrology? Is astrology only *mostly* fake? These are all legitimate questions.

Like *Sesame Street*, my mother fervently believes in knowledge and education being the only paths to success, so of *course* she loved a name that basically means *smarty-pants*.

Common mispronunciations range from the condonable UH-KILL-UH (which would make such a dope DJ name) to the you-didn't-even-try-at-all-comma-asshole pronunciation, ALKALINE. I also have vivid memories of watching *The Sandlot* and *Pee Wee's Big Adventure* as a kid and thinking it was super unfair how my name rhymed with something called tequila, which would later be known as my best frenemy.

I've never *hated* my name though. To me, it almost sounded like the name of a princess in a Disney movie. It had a beautiful ring to it coming out of even the grossest of mouths. But I did come close to hating it once. And I still have a vendetta against Keke Palmer.

In the spring of 2006, while I was slacking through the second semester of sophomore year of undergrad, a movie called *Akeelah and the Bee* came out. It starred Keke Palmer as eleven-year-old Ak*ee*lah, a spelling-bee champion-in-waiting in an inner city. Filled with family fun and Laurence Fishburne's encouragement, it made me completely sick. To begin, Akilah is spelled with one *I*, not fifty *E*s. Additionally, if a movie studio is going to blatantly steal my life story the very least they could do is change the main character's name.

That's right. I'm *pretty sure* that *Akeelah and the Bee* is based on my life. And not just because Akeelah stole my name—because I, too, was a spelling-bee queen.

In first grade I got a 100 percent on every spelling test Ms. Moore could throw at me. *On, an, sack, bat, back, black, snack.* My brain prioritized the spelling of *snack* the moment I found out which Dunk-a-Roos I liked best. The moment I saw a word in a book or heard a new word in conversation I committed its spelling to memory. I never had to study. I knew far too many words and their elementary spellings to be intimidated by a twenty-word quiz. I was promptly moved up to the third-grade spelling level, which, again, presented no challenge.

By fifth grade, word had spread that no one could out-spell Aki*l*ah in the upcoming school-wide spelling bee. It wasn't much of a reputation, but it sure beat the hell out of being the kid everyone suspected of hoarding milk cartons in his backpack. *Any* cred is better than that.

The air smelled fresher the morning of the bee. It was

unseasonably warm for spring, and the dew made the grass sparkle like the Emerald City. Waltzing pompously into the library, I didn't even wince at the ancient librarian with the toe thumb (google it), who was mumbling about returning books and permanent records or something.

I watched a girl who made fun of me back in my Boys & Girls Club days (for crying during the Halloween sleepover when they made six-year-old me watch *Scream*) misspell *prey* as she didn't even *think* to ask to hear it used in a sentence. I rubbed my little paws together as sticky kids misspelled *sanitary*, *cleanliness*, and *hygiene*.

The final round came, and suddenly my nerves showed up. I had to win. What excuse would I have for not winning? I was the girl who knew how to spell. Before I would even have to face my mom, I'd have to face my class at recess. Who knew how much they'd drag me if the girl who beat them every week in spelling lost to anyone else.

Mom's spaghetti. This *mattered*. When it got to be the last word, I took my mother's advice. *Take a deep breath. Slow down.* My word was *unnecessary*. Two *N*s, one *C*. Eat it, other kids! Akilah just won her way to the regional spelling bee.

I could hear excited screams from the other classrooms. I forgot this would be broadcast on our closed-circuit televisions. In that moment, I understood what it must feel like to be Harry Potter. Everyone had heard rumors about him and his damn lightning bolt scar, and they were probably incredulous or maybe even annoyed at how much buzz he had about him. But then, when put to the test, he saved the whole damn school and world. That was basically what I did, by spelling a word right on a sunny Wednesday in Kentucky.

The regional spelling bee was a big deal. We had to pile into the RAV4 and drive to Lexington, an hour away, early in the morning on a Saturday. The whole ride down was silent as I read through a tiny paperback book with the *official* spelling words for this round of the spelling bee. Page after page were words I knew already. If I didn't, I'd stare intently for ten seconds and then close my eyes and spell it out loud. Then I'd reopen my eyes, look to the little book, and find that I had already memorized the spelling. Some of the longer words came with definitions, but mostly the words had no homonyms and were never meant to be understood, only remembered.

"Remember to go slow and take a deep breath before you start," Mom reminded me.

Even if it had just worked a month prior, I hated this advice. I could fly through a twenty-word spelling quiz any day of the week, but now I had to stretch before I could flex?

"Yes ma'am," I said, because that's what you say when your mother tells you to do something. Otherwise, you run the risk of getting a seriously long "talking to" about how she didn't get this far in life by being stupid and maybe I'd make it that far if I stopped being stupid and talking back.

The regional spelling bee was to be televised on KET, the statewide public access channel. I'm not sure which family members would tune in, but I assumed everyone from my aunts, uncles, and their kids to the little boy from social studies class who inexplicably handed out coupons instead of Valentines that year would be watching. This made me immeasurably nervous. See, spelling was easy, but looking pretty, confident, and spelling words perfectly at a natural volume in a timely manner was a lot of pressure, and based on my previous on-camera experience, I wasn't entirely sure I was up to the challenge.

Just a couple years earlier a local TV channel had had auditions for a zoo correspondent. They were looking for charismatic, cute kids to share "news" from the Cincinnati Zoo and Botanical Garden in a weekly segment called "Kid's-Eye View from the Zoo." I'm not sure what news they were hoping for (this was many years before Harambe and Fiona the hippo), but I was convinced I should be the one to report it.

The line weaved through a room with live animals. Once it was your turn, you were seated with bright lights in your face and two cameras facing you and a strange adult white man who was holding a koala. I don't know if it was just the whole "talking to an adult stranger about my favorite cartoons," or the fact that when I went to pet the koala it was not even a little soft, or the pressure of having to be something special on camera for other people to see, but I froze. I couldn't think of any good cartoons even though I spent almost all of my free time in front of or wishing I was in front of a TV.

Suffice it to say I never recorded a news segment at the zoo because I wasn't offered the position. But I'm pretty sure the little blond boy they chose never wrote a book.

I pushed the thought away. I wasn't about to close up like a clam again. My mom thought I was a little star, and I mostly wanted her to keep believing that. Also it would be cool to rub it in my crappy fifth-grade teacher's face if I were to go to the state championships and *gasp* maybe even to the national spelling bee.

My hair looked good and my outfit was clean. Mom parked while I ran in to register.

"What's your name?"

"Akilah."

"Spell that."

I laughed at the woman in her best Wynonna Judd

costume. She didn't get it. Probably wasn't a speller, just a volunteer.

Joining the other kids in the front of the auditorium, I looked back to find my mom dropping her purse into an empty seat next to her. I waved. She waved. My heart rate was somewhere near "just ran a mile uphill in the sun." We had a half hour to talk to the other kids, but bump that. I wasn't there to make friends. I worried that if I made even one friend and they beat me I'd have to address that level of betrayal. This was fifth grade. I wasn't big enough yet to be the bigger person. No, I'd bite my tongue and try to remember the words from that damn pamphlet. Had I missed any pages?

"Will the first row of spellers please rise?" a voice boomed. I was in the second row so I did nothing but await further instruction.

"Form an orderly line. We will call you one at a time to the microphone. There we will give you a word. Please restate the word, then spell, and state the word again. If you spell the word correctly, go sit at the end of the second row of spellers. If you spell the word wrong . . ."

I stopped listening. She wasn't talking to me.

The first round went quickly. Apparently, I wasn't the only person with their heartbeat in their ears. Kid after kid dropped out. Maybe five of the first row of fifteen were still in the running. Soon enough I was called to the microphone.

"Spell *panic*."

I laughed, and the audience laughed. Good to know we were all on the same page.

"Panic: p-a-n-i-c. *Panic*."

"That's correct."

And all of the nerves fell away. Why did I think this was so tough? I smiled at the judges and went to the end of the second row. Round two would be upon us soon, but before that I had to look back and wave at my mom, again. She waved back.

Round two began like the other. I was eighth to go up. The kid ahead of me misspelled *muumuu* spectacularly. Halfway through he realized he had spelled it wrong and just started saying anything. I respected it. If you're going to burn out, you might as well burn bright. But now it was my turn.

I approached the microphone. Confident, no, *cocky*. Instead of worrying that I'd sound like a moron or say the wrong thing, I was already planning my outfits for the national spelling bee. The announcer said a word. So, instead of taking a deep breath or anything, I just spelled:

"Scandal: s-c-a-n-d-a-l. *Scandal*," I said, walking to take my seat at the end of the row to prepare for round three.

Halfway through my march I heard, "I'm sorry, the correct spelling was s-c-o-u-n-d-r-e-l. *Scoundrel*."

Disbelief, shock. I hardly even remembered where the disgraced bad spellers were supposed to go. I took one last look at the row of kids moving forward in the competition, but they wouldn't even look at me. I hung my head and held back tears as I found my mom, already holding her bag, ready to pile back in the car for the drive home.

"I *told* you to take a deep breath and wait, but no. You just rushed it. If you ever listened to me you'd have won." The speech I'll never forget. Even now Marilynn gets pissed off when I bring up the spelling bee. "A waste of gas," as it were.

At the close of freshman year at Berea College I had almost completely moved on from the mortifying spelling bee display. I'd gotten jobs, gotten into college, and could finally hear either s-c-word without the flush of latent shame. I had left behind my old identity, content to brag about my nail beds and other less academic gifts. I saw the trailer for *Akeelah and the Bee* during my afternoon ritual of watching *Oprah* and eating my microwave popcorn pre-dinner. Critics already loved it. Purposely earnest and heartwarming, it made me want to kick a wall.

From that point on, meeting people has been a painful experience.

"Like *Akeelah and the Bee*?" they all ask, proud of their clever word association.

"No," I answer without explanation. The alternative of me recounting the incidents of identity theft, PTSD (Post-Traumatic Spelling Disorder), and appearance-based envy would be breaking every bit of small talk etiquette.

My blood-feud with Keke, aka Broadway's Cinderella, extends to this very day. My nephew Mason had a hard time with "Kiwi" (my childhood nickname) as a baby and has taken up calling me "Kiki." It's really fucking adorable when he calls me "my Kiki," so I never corrected him.

But if Keke and I ever meet, I want her to know that though none of my names mean it, I forgive her. If she had known that her ten-year-old acting chops and family nickname were causing me such anguish, I'm sure she would have begged for the studio to scrap the film and suggested her own legal name change. Of course she would have—she'd have to be a downright narcissistic monster, so proud and absurd that she thinks her individual feelings far outweigh those of others only relevant due to absolute coincidence, to be picking this fight.

. . . Right?

Marilynn

I think you'd like my mom. She's not a cool mom in the *Mean Girls* sense—letting us drink in the house or trying to impress my friends—but she is cool. She has a solid record collection, she has a story for every occasion, she bought and is renovating a bus for nomadic travels, and she's the reason I have never taken anything too seriously. I've never laughed to the point of tears with anyone more.

Marilynn Elizabeth (named after Marilyn Monroe and Elizabeth Taylor, respectively) is the kind of mom who is always in my corner, even when it might be easier not to be. One very real thing I have in common with my mother (and grandmother) is horrible, small veins. If you tell a doctor that you have small veins, they'll accuse you of being a greedy wuss, of wanting to use the supply of small needles designed for children for yourself.

They will then proceed to try to draw blood with the giant needles they used for André the Giant and Dwayne "The Rock" Johnson. This will prove futile and excruciating. They will "blow" the vein and bruise your entire arm. Then, as if it's your first rodeo, they will exclaim, "Wow! You really *do* have small veins!" and sheepishly retrieve the petite needles. They will then proceed to stab you no less than three more times on either arm, finally resigning themselves to vampirically removing your life juice from the most painful spot—your hand.

As an adult it's enough to piss you off, but as a kid with little agency it just makes you howl, pathetically drenching your face and T-shirt while confused as to why this situation is still happening dear god make it stop!

My mom would always schedule her blood work around when I had to go so we could hold each other through the pain. *Yes*, it is truly so bad that we have a familial tradition surrounding doctors hurting us.

The worst time was when I was in an asthma medication study—the kind from the radio commercials. For a payment of three hundred dollars, I'd try brand-new steroids for lung development and asthma relief. Since albuterol wasn't working (and recently a study came out saying that albuterol doesn't work at the same rate for black people . . . shock sur-fucking-prise) I had nothing to lose, but plenty of rage and weight to gain.

After the first month of taking the oral steroid, I had gained about twenty pounds on my four-foot-two frame. I was a little smiley face in a sea of bony third graders. Every month I'd have to get blood work to make sure nothing else had changed dramatically. This particular time they never found the smaller needles and never actually figured out how to get the blood out of my body. I suppose since they were already hurting me so much they could have just used a saber to cut me in half and drain whatever they could into a variety of tubes, but instead they just gave up after my bloodcurdling screams prompted one family to leave the waiting room and another single older man to give me a twenty-dollar bill to "calm down." It was a whole-ass fiasco.

My mom felt so awful about the whole ordeal that she took me to Wendy's. It was the '90s, so fast food was absolutely beyond acceptable as a gift. She even let me get the large, cup-holder-size Mountain Dew. This was perhaps a shade too far, as neither of us realized just how long the drive back to the school where both my mother works and I was being taught would be.

About twenty-five minutes into the trip I realized I had to pee, but my mom had already done so much to make the day up to me, I didn't want to ask to pull over. Before you tell me, *yes*, I know now that that was stupid. When you're a kid you do all kinds of irrational shit to be what you think is polite, or "good," or convenient. Turns out bodies don't care how thoughtful you *think* you are, and about ten minutes later the involuntary moaning began.

"Akilah, is that you?" my mom asked, genuinely concerned that perhaps she was having a stroke if I didn't also hear the guttural groans that came in fifteen-second increments.

"I have to pee!" I finally screamed. I couldn't pretend any longer. My arms were sore, my stomach was full of lime-green soda, and this was an emergency.

"God damn it, there's not an exit for five more minutes. You gotta hold it, baby." She tried to console me. I already knew this was going to be a nightmare. I tried to focus on dry things I'd read about in books: tundras, deserts, the Great Plains. *Sarah, Plain and Tall*. When you're little your worldview isn't even big enough to help in scenarios like this.

My mom sped off the exit and to a gas station. I hopped out of the car as she ran to the cashier to get the restroom key. But . . . it just wasn't enough.

I gave up. She was running back to the car when I

pulled down my shorts and underwear and then just peed right on top of them.

"NO! KILAH, NO! OH MY GOD!"

The stream lasted for the greater part of two minutes. Cars on the highway passed my moon.

Mom found a towel in the trunk and laid it down for me to sit on. The rest of the ride back to school was a lecture on the importance of pulling your panties and bottoms to the side if you have to use the restroom. I couldn't see how this knowledge would be helpful seeing as I'd just died of embarrassment.

When we got back to the school, I half expected to have my mom announce over the intercom that her youngest daughter peed her pants today. I don't know why I thought she'd do that, but I was so embarrassed. I was embarrassed for her. She told her assistant, Susan, what happened, and I was just waiting for a break in the discussion for me to apologize again for being born. But she wasn't disappointed. She was *laughing*. She was laughing so hard she had to take her glasses off to wipe the tears out of her eyes.

"Worse shit always happens," she assured me. I've moved with that energy ever since.

A couple months passed and the asthma trial medicine was really doing a number. I was still a chubby bean, but I had the new added benefit of mood swings. One such swing came out at the wrong time. We were in the middle of an after-school-program kickball game.

For the second time in this essay, I'm too uncomfortable not to preface with *yes, I know there was an adult solution to the problem, but I was an irrational child at the time.*

Crap, I do *not* want to tell you about this. Anyway.

One afternoon we were playing kickball in the after-school program. I was not athletic, but it was before I realized I could decline such an invitation. Our team had amassed two outs. A mean girl with a high ponytail pitched the ball to me, and as it rolled and bounced I thought, *If I can just not get out immediately, that will satisfy my friends. That'll be enough.*

I couldn't decide if I should hold my breath or take deep breaths, and by the time I decided on the latter I had kicked the ball. Far! And no one caught it. It bounced somewhere in the "outfield" of our concrete playground. And I ran! I ran as fast as I my short legs would carry me.

First base seemed like a given, but I got cocky and kept it moving, and by some miracle the outfielder overthrew the ball to the third baseman. I was cocky, but not a moron, and I decided to park it on second base. My team, once seated on this concrete barrier, was now on their feet, cheering me on. The second baseman was in disbelief. *This girl?* She's *the one who kicked a double?* Yes, bitch, IT WAS ME. You shoulda picked me to be on your team when we had time for all that, but it's no use worrying. It was time for Michael to kick for our team.

Every school has a Michael. He's not only the fastest kid by a measurable amount, but he also spends all summer playing for neighborhood peewee teams in prep for the school year's football, basketball, baseball, and soccer offerings. He was the captain of all the teams. It was assumed that he'd be the closer for the game, and I was ready to go.

The high-ponytail girl looked at me as if she was gonna do that thing baseball players do trying to tag out the sad sack who leans too far off the base. Sadly for her, I wasn't going anywhere. I could have just had one foot on the base, but I was fully planted. I was not going to be the reason my team lost. I get it, she had underestimated my newfound kicking talent, but hoping I would make some other mistake just feels like denial, even typing it up now. Girl, I was dope, you should've recognized.

Back to the game: The high pony decided to give up on her plan and pitched the ball to Michael. I couldn't see her face, but I'm guessing the expression was crestfallen mixed with rage. The stakes couldn't have felt higher, even though there were no prizes for whichever team won, just bragging rights. It couldn't have mattered less, but what else did we have to worry about? This may as well have been an Olympic finals game.

Michael kicked the ball over the fence that separated the school from the poor neighbors who probably underestimated how loud the kids would be all day and late into the afternoon. Another ball kicked into their yards, another plea with the universe to help them find literally anywhere else to live. It was a certified home run.

So I ran! And even having a two-base head start, Michael was closing in. Still, I "hustled" to home plate, and even did a cute little hop. I high-fived everyone while Michael came to the base right behind me. We won! Eat it, high ponytail and other people I've forgotten.

As we were celebrating, the outfield team had retrieved the ball and the pitcher with the ponytail came up to our celebration and threw the ball at me. Hard. The ball was the same light rubber one you remember, but it hit me in the stomach and even though it *didn't* hurt, her intention was to hurt me. My whole team turned to figure out what she was thinking.

"You're out!" she screamed, her desperation for the game to go into further innings on display.

"You didn't touch the base," she continued, not

specifying which base. At this point the program coordinator should have probably stepped in to tell her that's not how home runs work, and that because the ball went so far we just scored two points, ending the game and her hopes for a college kickball scholarship. Tough cookies, kid. Movies rarely show the losing teams, but surely you'll figure out what to do with all that rage.

What HP (high pony) hadn't realized was that I was out of my mind on the asthma-study steroids. Even *I* couldn't articulate that it was not only bananas that she hit me after the game was called, but that in any event we could have just done a re-kick, with me on second base. Michael was sure to sink it deep into the outfield again, and she'd just have to come closer to terms with her inevitable defeat. Instead, I railed into her.

"Fuck you! Fuck YOU! I'm not out, motherfucker! Your team sucks and you suck and your mom is ugly! Fuck you! At least I don't live in those shitty apartments with all the roaches! You're jealous because my mom is pretty!"

This was a lot and, rightly, reduced the girl to tears. But not just her; I have always had that problem of getting so mad that I am also screaming and crying. When I die, if there is a God and she's taking requests, I'd like to see this interaction again. I'm not proud of how I acted, but I think it still would be kinda funny to watch a third grader's 'roid rage as an adult. Kids are just exploding emotions.

Before anyone could grab me, I ran back to the building, into my mom's office. I was crying and screaming.

"What's wrong, Kilah?"

"And I told her that at least my mom's not ugly and that our house is better! Fuck!" And my mom tried to hide her laughter. This was uncomfortable because I was a raving lunatic, but also because that other girl's mom also worked at the school, and happened to be in my mother's office, and my mother had already agreed to give them a ride home that day.

Things were awkward. What was the right move? Cancel the car ride and do the Triple-X hip thrust at high pony and her mom? My mom had to think fast, as high pony was about to walk into her office.

So she yelled at me.

"Kilah! That is not nice. You need to apologize to her right now. Are you ashamed of yourself? Because I'm ashamed of you," and then to HP's mom, "I'm so sorry, Brenda. I don't know what's gotten into her." And with that, she walked me to the bathroom to help me "fix my face."

I rinsed all the tears off, but before I could dry my face I replaced them with fresh rage tears.

"We won the game! This is so stupid!"

"Hush! You can't talk to people like that, Kilah. I'm giving them a ride home tonight!"

"Why?!"

"I told them way before that I would. You can't just lose your temper on people."

I rolled my eyes and went and sat in my mom's back seat. I stared out the window, waiting for the uncomfortable twenty-minute car ride to begin. *I'm not going to apologize*, I'd reckoned. *I'm not gonna punk out and apologize.*

The car ride was spent with my mopey face pressed against the glass. No one spoke, the radio played R & B. When we pulled up to their complex, my mom turned down the radio. Before she would just let them go on with their lives, she made me apologize one more time.

"I'm sorry I said your mom is ugly. Your mom is not ugly."

It wasn't a great apology. If I had to grade it, I'd give it a C-minus. I believe in being specific when apologizing, but bringing up someone's mom's attractiveness or lack thereof *again* is just not a great move. Still, it was the most civility I could muster. If I had my way I woulda lunged across the car and choked the girl until her mom unbuckled her seat belt and got her out of there. I'm just being real. The steroids on top of the well of rage, the supposedly "lost game," and my fall from grace in slow motion had me unprepared for reconciliation in the slightest.

"It's all right," they both said. It wasn't, and it went without saying that since the car ride was so awkward it probably wouldn't be happening again. There was always the city bus? Eh, no one felt good about that afternoon.

This would be the last year I spent at my mom's school. It was her decision. It wasn't because of the kickball blowup. It was just that Latonia Elementary School had the only "gifted and talented" program in the district and I'd passed the test to get in with flying colors. I was nervous because I'd amassed a pretty solid group of friends that I'd known since preschool, and changing up the rotation this close to puberty was a risk.

The summer before I made the switch, my mom found ways for me to work off the 'roid rage. For starters, we dropped out of the study. So far my asthma had not improved and my attitude was worse off. But she also enrolled me, Lanie, and Bo in the local chapter of the National Junior Tennis League. In the back of the RAV4, vibing out to "Electric Avenue" on cassette, we'd make the journey from Florence to Covington in the midst of smog alerts to learn how to play tennis from Mr. Johnson.

Venus and Serena really came into national focus that

year, and my mom thought that Lanie and I had a chance at being the next generation. Spoiler alert: it absolutely did not happen. The most active I am is trying to put on a sports bra to then sit on my couch and think about working out, and Lanie, well, same. Bo just liked activities, so he came along.

Maybe my favorite thing about my mom is that she doesn't take anything seriously, so when Coach Johnson would say, "Uh-kill-uh! Get ya rack back!" she would laugh hysterically in her car and quote it the whole way home. We'd worked on our volley skills and eventually I learned exactly one trick, which is serving the ball without even looking at it. It's only ever been impressive one time, in college, and after that I got a leg cramp and forfeited.

But my mom has always wanted all of us to be well-rounded. We did so many activities: soccer, band, speech and drama, tennis, webbies, the talent show. We were poor, but we never felt poor, because my mom was adamant about finding free or very cheap things for us to do and learn. Maybe it's because she finished her degree in her thirties, or because she saw how the world opened up for my sister Tasha when she went to Stanford for undergrad. Back then, I don't think I really appreciated all the time my mom had scheduled away from my beloved couch and TV set. I was a person who liked the idea of doing things, but the act of doing things a lot less.

I struggle to imagine what kind of person I'd turn out to be if my mom was less passionate or ambitious on my behalf. I used to feel bad for myself, like, "poor me, I wish my mom would just butt out and let me be sedentary," but now that I am my own boss, I try to keep myself motivated. To try new things rather than trying nothing. And suffice it to say I have my mother to thank for that. Perhaps I'm not a perfect musician (though I *am* using an app to learn how to play piano, so in your face, traditional way of doing things), and I never became a star athlete. But I stopped being afraid to try because I had someone in my corner who believed in me even when I couldn't see that for myself.

I think you'd like my mom. I really do.

George

A guy makes a Twitter joke. It's about "daddy issues" and women who "have them." He thinks he's clever, and eleven retweets and twenty-eight faves affirm him. Women with fathers who treat them poorly—that's the whole joke. Who'd ever love them?

I didn't go to my father's funeral. I stayed at home and ate KFC mashed potatoes and gravy and watched *Mad Men* seasons one and two on Netflix. I maintain that this was the better decision.

A few days after my dad died, I got my wisdom teeth removed. I only had three, which is supposedly more common than you'd think. When I came to, the doctor was hugging my mom and telling her I'd be just fine. My mom (rightly) found this display to be super weird. Why was this old man in a white coat hugging her body? And why *wouldn't* I have been fine? It was a routine surgery with an incredibly high survival rate. On the Sunday of my father's funeral, I found out I had developed a pretty gnarly infection and had to be placed on antibiotics. Maybe the doctor really *did* know something we didn't.

When I called my boss at the water company, Charlie, to tell him my dad died, I was startled by my eyes suddenly wetting and my voice cracking.

"Oh my goodness. Akilah. I am so, *so* sorry. Take all the time you need. Don't even worry about anything. Just be with your family and take care of yourself," Charlie told me.

I wasn't on the verge of tears because I was sad about losing a parent; I wanted to cry because I was so relieved. For the first time in more than a decade and a half, I felt a weight lifted. It was over. *He* was over. He couldn't hurt our family anymore. I wanted to cry for the greener pastures his death represented. For my mom who'd been tricked with twenty-five years of lies. For my brother who needed a father who really *saw* him, you know? And a dad who could be someone worth looking up to. For my sister Lanie whose mood ebbed and flowed with his mercurial affection and lack thereof. For me, and all my helpless rage. I needed to cry for all of them.

Warped Tour 2011 was the hottest day of my life. My friend McKenna made good use of her metallic green VW Beetle and drove us to Riverbend—the outdoor music venue of choice in Cincinnati—for the annual event. The air was thick and humid and nasty. It was like being dipped in nacho cheese. We spent most of the day in a haze, bumping into friends and emptying our bank accounts on lukewarm bottled water. As the more invested pop-punk fan, I convinced McKenna to stay just long enough to watch Gym Class Heroes, a band whom I had met and befriended six years earlier at the same concert series, take the stage. Their live performances are electrifying and would make all the sweat and headaches worth it, I promised her.

We stayed and the performance was one of the best of the day. We jumped up and down in the front row, and the band came and sang right in our faces. I took so many pictures and videos. Our headaches subsided, and being surrounded by the B.O. of thousands of people in Vans sneakers stopped grating on our nerves. As the band left the stage, we made a beeline for the Beetle and decided that Chili's would be the dinner/decompression spot for the evening.

As we scanned the menus, my phone rang. It was my mom.

"Do you mind if I take this?"

"Nah, it's cool," McKenna assured me.

And then our conversation went like this:

"So . . . Your father died today."

"Oh?"

"Yeah."

"Hmph. Well, that's kind of perfect because I have the wisdom teeth appointment Friday, so the bereavement leave from work will give me, like, the full week off."

"Yeah. You should call your sister. She seemed pretty upset. Bo just stared out of the car window when I told him. He couldn't look at me."

"Hmm. Okay. I'm at dinner. I'll be home later. Love ya, bye!"

"Love ya, bye!"

As I hung up, I took notice of McKenna's expression. Her giant blue eyes looked even more impossibly huge as she asked me what happened.

"Oh! My dad's dead," I said, probably too nonchalantly.

"What? Are you okay?" she checked.

"Yeah, dude, it's fine. I think I'm gonna get this fajita rollup thing . . ." I said. And that was that.

The Sunday before George Elmer died, I joked to my mother that if he was gonna go soon, this week would be ideal. With the surgery and the music festival taking up two days, this would be the only way to get the full week off of work. In hindsight, humor was the only way we could ever talk about what my father had done. My wit and cynicism came from a place of being overwhelmed by years of sadness and circumstance. Finding the light was the only way to survive.

I was nineteen and very much in love the summer that I met Elita. My boyfriend dragged his blond Southern charm to the Greater Cincinnati Area to stay with me for a week. It was incredibly romantic. In an attempt to make and save a little money, we took jobs at the "Taste of Cincinnati," a two-day event, handing out promotional flavored water. Five hundred dollars for a day and a half of handing out water was the best gig in town, and we made a really great team. He spent his time changing out the ice and lifting twenty-four packs of mango-strawberry and pomegranate-açaí bottles while I explained to overheated tourists that this entire flavor really *was* available for zero sugar or calories.

On our final day of working, our legs ached, we were sweaty, and we just wanted to go home. That's when she approached. A girl, maybe a couple inches taller than me, with familiar high cheekbones and a beauty mark in the

middle of her clavicles, just like mine. We both knew immediately, but she asked to make sure.

"Are you my sister?" she asked so faintly I'm surprised
I heard it.

"Is George Hughes your dad?" I countered.

"Yeah. This is so weird," she said. And I handed her a
sample of the mango-strawberry water.

I knew she was real.

The last conversation I ever had with my father was at three
a.m. on the phone. He called me back after I left him a scathing voicemail on his answering machine. Since I knew he
had an answering machine, I knew his wife would hear the
message as I left it. In it, I detailed how pathetic he was.
How bad I felt for his wife who stuck with him, knowing
all the while that he was a sociopath. How she babysat us
as kids and I'm grateful that she didn't poison me and my
siblings knowing what she knew. How insanely pathetic it
was that he lied about the girl who reached out to me on
Facebook, asking if I was his daughter. How pathetic it was
that he *denied* his other children to my mother, as if that
would somehow make anything better.

He called me back, and I answered promptly. Before
I could say, "Hello?" he called me a tramp, and I genuinely

laughed into the receiver, almost dropping the phone from my body convulsing at his lack of self-awareness. I told him how ironic I found it that *he* was the one with a million kids and a bunch of families and maintaining that lie for nearly thirty years, but *I'm* the tramp. Priceless.

The last thing he ever said to me was "I'm going to come to your house and kill you. You're going to die tonight, bitch."

I smiled, considering this.

"I'd like to see your old ass try."

And that was that.

Summer 2007 was an equally bad and good time in my life. I loved my friends and my retail job at the mall. I was at war with my body, and an older boy I knew from high school did something unforgivable to me when I had a sleepover with his sister. It haunted me every night for a few years. The only person I told about it was him, the boy who did it. I asked him what the fuck he was thinking. Why would he do that to me? He told me he was fucked up. That his dad wasn't around and it made him crazy; that the hole where his father should be rotted within him and that was the reason for his sociopathic tendencies. That was obviously B.S. Both our dads sucked, but only one of us was a supreme creep.

That July I lost a lot of weight from being too sad to eat and sleeping upwards of fifteen hours a day when not working at the store. This was the second time in my life that I thought I might die young.

At some point that summer, Lanie told me that Dad had been diagnosed with bone cancer. She said he was looking thin, that she thought he was going to die.

I told her I didn't care. I didn't.

Finals week of the first semester of my sophomore year at college was tough. I was clinically depressed, exhausted, and pulling all-nighters for days at a time. I showed up to my campus position at Media Services wearing the same outfit two days in a row. No one noticed.

At around two a.m. that Tuesday in 2006, I got a phone call, which was unusual in the lonely days of winter. I took the call in bed, since my roommate was out of town and I wasn't disturbing anyone. It was Mom.

"Lanie is hysterical right now. She left me a voicemail and I don't know what it means. She was just crying and screaming. I might have to go to Morehead . . . something about a message on Facebook?"

She was worried. I was worried. I opened a tab in Firefox and clicked to Facebook. I had a new message.

I read it aloud, not thinking it might be best to keep it to myself for a day or so:

> Hey my name is Elita and I just found out that I have some brothers name Chephren, Mark, George and Bolani [*sic*]. I go to Wright State and I was just wondering if you were related also. I was told I had two more sisters one that went to Berea and one that go [*sic*] to Morehead. I would love to hear from you!!!!

The phone line went silent. It was the kind of silence that you can actually hear. If this moment had occurred in a movie, it would have been written into the script, followed by a gasp and sad piano or strings. It was the sound of two hearts breaking simultaneously for the exact same reason.

"Whoa," I whispered. I knew my father hadn't been there for me growing up, but I didn't realize he hadn't been there for three families' worth of children. I realized that my mother didn't know—that if she had known, I wouldn't even be alive.

I hated him.

They mispronounced my name at high school graduation and I refused to cross the stage until they said it right. I was the only student representative to the Board of

Education in the commonwealth. I had pictured the finality of high school often in the weeks prior. None of my fantasies included the principal fumbling over the eleven syllables encompassed in my name. I also didn't imagine that my father would choose not to attend my graduation.

This was the day I decided to stop excusing the decisions of bad people.

The principal finally got it right on try 2.5, and I walked across the stage and hugged each member of the Board of Education and waved to my mom.

Dad came over to our house on my eleventh birthday. I remember opening the front door with a big smile. We'd hug, and he'd tell me happy birthday and notice how much I'd grown. Then he'd hand me my gift.

I went in to hug him, and he didn't hug back. At least, not really. I looked up at him and said, "I'm so excited!"

"Huh. Why?" he asked, clueless.

"Because it's my birthday!" I continued, expectantly.

"Oh. Well . . . happy birthday, Kiwi," he added, detached. I stood my ground and smiled, not getting it.

"You look kind of short, li'l bit. Where's your mom?"

And that was that.

On my fifth birthday, my mom told me to pick up the

upstairs telephone. I ran into Tasha's room and obliged. *It was him.*

"Your mom says you have a song for me," he said lovingly.

"Sing the song, Kilah!" Mom pleaded. I smiled from ear to ear, singing "You Are My Sunshine" at full outdoor-voice volume. I heard him clap on the other line.

"That was beautiful, Kiwi," he said. I didn't realize that he had ruined that birthday until years later.

I'm four years old and wearing a navy blue cardigan with gold buttons down the front. Lanie is dressed just the same. It's windy and I think I might blow away on the walk from Mom's car up to his front door. Lanie and I hold hands. Ms. Laura lets us in through the screen door. We wave goodbye to Mom.

We spend two nights at his house. He makes fun of my inability to eat foods that touch. He asks me if it's okay that he makes me a sandwich with the bread touching the cheese. We only see him at dinnertime.

I stand on the enclosed patio outside his kitchen and watch his boxer, Dewey, chase butterflies around the yard. I'm scared to meet him, but I like watching him run around freely and like that he comes up to the bottom part of the screen door to meet my face when I try and fail to whistle for him. If my dad has this, he must be good. Only good people get this.

Ms. Laura re-braids our hair and gives us a bath. She kisses our foreheads before bed and when we leave the next day, she gives us dolls to take home. I'm buckled into the leather back seat watching the teal analog on his car's radio as funk music plays. I look out the window to the highway. There's an old company that has a sign that's a tin man who appears to be running in slow motion halfway between his house and ours back across the river. I think about it until I fall asleep. I wake up in my mom's arms, being put down in my bottom bunk. Things are peaceful. Everyone is innocent.

I log on to Twitter and read the tweet about daddy issues. I read hundreds of tweets like it every year. I unfollow and block without remorse.

Where to Say Your Dad Lives When He's Dead

"Hell, but I'm not sure which circle."

"Underground."

"Depends on what you believe."

"On a farm upstate with all the other dogs."

"Bad memories mostly."

"He doesn't."

The Little Cheerleader
That Couldn't

Never have I ever seen an episode of the '90s hit *90210*. If you'd told me that one day I'd be at the Sundance Episodic Story Lab and asked if I'd seen it by one of the writers of the show while it was in its prime, and that I'd subsequently lie and say I had seen it, I probably wouldn't have believed you. Still, it happened, and I responded with "yes."

I didn't expect a follow-up question, and none came. Why would it? Everyone else there had seen the show and was aware of its place in pop culture history. Had he asked who my favorite characters were, I'd have answered, "Flapjack and Suzie, respectively." If those are characters on the show, then I'd continue to bullshit why their teen tribulations spoke to me (at the tender age of five while the show originally aired). If they were not characters, as I suspect, I'd just admit that my intersection with the show does not extend beyond the theme song, but that theme song was incredibly important to me.

If you play the first eight notes and the important *clap clap* afterward, I will immediately be transported back to Ninth District Elementary School, a formative home for me from ages three to eight. My mother works at the school as a family resource center coordinator whose job ranges from getting vouchers for less fortunate students to buy things like clothes, shoes, and school supplies to putting on the annual Readifest, which is an entire festival that sees dentists, hairdressers, and teachers in dunk tanks prepare students for the next school year. Marilynn always liked to work late, so Lanie, Bo, and I spent after-school time roaming the halls, finding other kids with whom to loiter.

One fateful day I made my way to the hallway outside my mom's office that had a little alcove where kids would line up in the morning and be walked to their classrooms. Instead of cross-legged first graders, there were about twelve fourth through sixth graders with high ponies tied with colorful scrunchies and big, puffy bangs awaiting instruction from Meredith Teddy, a preschool attendant and the school's cheerleading coach.

I knew Meredith Teddy because she had daughters the same age as me and Lanie: Jenny and Jaime. Like my mother, Meredith Teddy had gotten tired of explaining that Jenny and Jaime weren't twins. With bright red hair, matching outfits and freckles, and expensive gymnastics training, they were our sworn nemeses. The preschool wasn't big enough for more than one cute duo, and Lanie and I were ready for the challenge.

Regardless of my one-sided vendetta, Mrs. Teddy was always pretty nice to me. Her kids got picked up by their father after school while she taught the cheerleaders, and it was the sound of the *90210* theme song that first caught my attention. The cheer squad sat in front of chairs that would be used at the pep rally and during halftime at the school's basketball games. I popped a squat and watched, amazed at the choreography and how cool and adult everyone seemed.

Duh-nuh-nuh-nuh, duh-nuh-nuh-nuh, clap clap. The girls ran to chairs that were supposed to, in effect, look like they were riding in a car. Two girls knelt in front, while the one on the left pretended to be turning a steering wheel. Their ponytails flipped side to side with their miming. When I was a kid, I truly believed that I saw that car, cup holders and roll-up windows and all. It seemed so magical, so girly. I wanted in desperately.

After a while I got up, still standing pretty close to the wall so as not to be noticed, and mimicked the dance movements. *Five, six, seven, eight, neck roll, snap, walk-walk-skip, sit on the chair, head left, head right, head down, arms up!* I memorized the hell out of that dance. If Vine had been alive in the '90s, I would have become a meme. There were no black cheerleaders on the team, but my little preschool butt was keeping in time and step with all the blonde hair and neon.

I became an unofficial member of the squad about a month later. Mrs. Teddy had noticed me putting in *the work* with the squad and taking water breaks with all the girls. I never got a uniform, but my mom got wind of my excitement and scheduled for us to attend the first basketball game where they'd debut the routine.

The cheerleaders found their spot out of bounds to the left of the bleachers, and I found a spot that was close to that, careful not to obscure them. We were a *team* and this performance wasn't just about me. Meredith would call out the name of a cheer and I'd get into my own solo formation, awaiting an older girl calling out, "Ready? Okay!"

Once I was old enough to try out for the cheerleading squad, I did. Fourth grade at Latonia Elementary School, and wouldn't you know it, Meredith Teddy was now *their* cheerleading coach. The tryouts were a week long, and the entire time they tested for things like how loud you can yell, if you can tumble, choreography, general ability to smile under any and all circumstances, etc. I couldn't tumble. I couldn't do a toe touch, or a back handspring, or a herkie, or any of the jumpy parts of cheerleading, but no one could touch me on the choreo. I was teaching it to other girls there by the third day.

Mrs. Teddy even took note of my deep alto voice.

"Love that yell, Kiwi!" she called, assuring me. I could picture the next week, having to change my AIM username to something about cheerleading, sitting at the popular-girl lunch table just talking about popularity, wearing matching scrunchies, and deciding once and for all who the better boyfriend would be, Dylan or Brandon.

The day of the tryouts was like any other. A bread-tangle of pizza with corn for lunch. Watching kids who understood the rules of Pokémon cards at recess. Waiting for the afternoon announcements. Soon I was wandering to the wall outside the music room, waiting my turn to audition. The hallway was too quiet, with girls so nervous that it seemed like they were being lined up for something far more sinister with less of an emphasis on cheer. Privately I considered how I couldn't afford not to make the team. I was the only black kid in my class, so I was already at a disadvantage socially (see chapter entitled "The South"). I couldn't afford to buy both the pastel and the metallic gel pens to make up the cool points. My mom thought Lunchables were a scam, so I couldn't even get a reputation as the girl who gave away her Capri Sun. I often brought pudding as the dessert for my lunch. Nobody *likes* pudding. We tolerate it, like we tolerate room-temperature soda and ingrown hairs. Would we take any other option if there was one? Yes.

I could see the other girls' minds working on this same problem. We were only ten years old, but we knew the social hierarchy. Pretty girls who do girly things and are generally seen as dainty always come out on top. If you ever challenge them you're just a big meanie, the grade school equivalent of a total bitch. I tried to get out of my head. Shake it out. You know this, Hughes. You've done it forty-five times. Your voice is deeper than all the other girls', just hit 'em with that "Ready? Okay!" and if they ask you to do a back handspring, change the subject.

"Number fourteen?" a voice called.

My cue. I sauntered into the room, practically marching. Head up, smile on, bring it.

It went fine. When they asked me to do a roundoff, I

just didn't. How can that be a deal breaker in the fourth grade? It just wouldn't make sense.

The protocol was put to us that someone would call tonight letting you know if you made the team or not. I got in the car and gushed to my mom, replaying all of the excitement of walking, clapping, and yelling.

"And then I yelled, 'Ready? Okay!' and I really *was* ready, okay," I recounted.

The moment I got home I made sure all the phones were on their chargers. We absolutely *would not* be missing this phone call because a phone was dead or missing. Bo would insist that that was "bullshit, man" because he really wanted to talk to a girl from class, but high school love would have to wait. If I didn't get a phone call, I could kiss goodbye all the goodbye kisses in my future. Who would ever love a girl who *wasn't* on the cheer squad?

Hours passed. It approached "rudely late" to call. My mom tried to comfort me, but I couldn't believe it. Who else at the tryouts had been ready for this moment for more than half their lives? It was too late to call around to hear who else didn't make the squad. I'd just have to go in the next day and pretend it was fine.

I was devastated. I lay facedown on my bed, ugly crying, not even caring that my whole shirt was wet with tears.

Oh, how unfair life is! It's not my fault I can't do a roundoff. Why would the audition be hinged on a skill you can't really learn in a week anyway? It's not like the whole team does a roundoff during the halftime show. I knew all the moves, on beat, backward and forward. I was made to cheer! My whole life had been leading up to this moment, mom's spaghetti, and somehow it wasn't enough.

When my mom dropped me off the next morning, all the other kids were talking about who made the team and who didn't. If I wasn't super close with the group, I'd tell them I didn't even try out. If I did I'd tell them that it was rigged. I tried out two more years at the school, and still didn't make it.

One day on the ride home from speech and drama in high school, my mom asked how the day was.

"Oh, they were holding cheerleading tryouts all week in the gym, so people just kept talking about that." Trying to denote that it was kind of a sore subject.

"Well, you know you never made the team because of me," she said, like I knew that already.

"Come again?"

"Mrs. Teddy. She and I go way back, and let's just say we haven't always seen eye to eye on things," she revealed.

"Huh," I considered. "So it wasn't the tumbling?"

"No, Kilah. Have you seen those cheerleaders? How many of them do you think are doing a flip?"

In hindsight it was only like two girls at the front who could do anything resembling gymnastics. The rest sort of marched and posed and smiled close to the beat.

"Damn," I said, somehow not vindicated by the meritless appointments of the other cheerleaders.

It turns out you can be excellent, objectively, at any number of things, and life will come in hot with the unfairness. To Mrs. Teddy's credit, she was never mean to me and never let on, but I internalized years of not being pretty enough, or white enough, or skinny enough because I couldn't figure out why I couldn't be that girl.

Now when I look back on my school years, I can't imagine how different my life would be if I had been a cheerleader. No one looks at me now and would even suspect that I had dreams of being that girl. That I insisted on watching cheer competitions any time they were on ESPN. That I've seen *Bring It On* more than five times and *The Godfather* less than one (it's just really long and I can't be everything to everybody).

And had I made the team, knowing what I now know about Mrs. Teddy, all of that doubt and self-hatred probably would have been made worse.

Besides, I won so many trophies competing in speech

and drama and now I can point to high school as a training ground for my current life, where I'm constantly in front of people speaking and making jokes. And our cheerleading team never won anything.

Fifth Grade Is a Scam

Like many children in the '90s, I was considered "gifted and talented." Do I believe I was smarter than most other kids? I don't know. The work didn't bother me, and I tended to get good grades, but being good at memorizing things has only helped me in adulthood for auditions and nothing else.

Back-to-school is my favorite season. Not only did my birthday often fall right smack in the middle of all the hoopla, but it feels like the universe giving you another chance at resolutions. Maybe in January I wasn't ready to change, but every school year can be different from the last. I liked picking an outfit from my new clothes. I loved the smell of fresh school supplies. I thought there was no higher calling than deciding which notebook and folder went with which class. My Trapper Keeper might as well have been a Mercedes-Benz. Before the first day of school I always had a hard time sleeping. The anticipation was on par with Christmas Day. Who had gotten taller? Who had a good story to tell about their summer? Who would want to hear about my Barbie car washes and tree-climbing?

In third grade I switched from the school my mother works at to Latonia Elementary School. It was the only school in the district with a program dedicated to high-achieving children, and it was a lot different from Ninth District.

I instantly noticed the lack of melanin in my new school. Lanie had gone to fourth grade there already and was entering fifth when I got there. There was one other black girl in my grade, and one biracial boy, but that was it. A far cry from classrooms with kids from everywhere at my old school. None of the faculty and staff was darker than a paper bag. Don't get me wrong, I'd noticed I was black before, it was just this was the first time I realized that some people assumed that was a bad thing.

To their credit, most kids didn't seem fazed by it at all. The biggest difference between the schools was the work-load. At Latonia I'd have homework every night, for at least an hour. This was good for me, because I was *so* bored not *having* to do anything. The schoolwork never stumped me.

I joined the A Honor Roll as soon as it was an option and tried a few after-school activities. I finished the year with a perfect record, new friends, and a hope for repeated success the next year.

That summer sucked. My grandmother died, and none of us took it well. Even now I don't know what "taking it well" looks like when someone who is in your life every day suddenly isn't. But that summer was incredibly difficult. I spent a lot of time alone, crying, but trying not to stress my mom out for any reason. When school rolled back around I was relieved to have something besides abject sadness to occupy my time.

Little did I know I was about to meet my archnemesis, the woman who would make my fifth-grade life hell: Ms. Murphy. To put it bluntly, we did not get along. I thought she was racist; she thought I was out to get her.

Our first of many classes in the day was gym, and our teacher, Mr. Dweeble, was basically an overly tan WWF wrestler from the '80s. In fourth grade I remember him telling the class that if we wanted to stay skinny (?) we should only eat bacon (???). In hindsight, how on earth? We were little kids? About to hit puberty? And he just gave some unsolicited diet advice? I *couldn't even* then, and I *can't even* now.

In the gym everything was red and tan. Like in most Kentucky elementary schools I've visited, the gym doubled as an auditorium, so there was a cape-esque red curtain that was open, revealing old personal trampolines and inflatable balls with handles that would be a hot commodity come recess. We did some "stretching," which was more like flopping our arms around and failing to reach our toes, and then we were asked to run five laps around the gym.

It was at that moment that I realized two things: (1) I needed a sports bra or any kind of bra honestly, because there were boobs and they were bouncing, and (2) my shoes squeaked. At the time the former seemed far more urgent than the latter. No one else had boobs yet. I needed to blend in with my less shapely peers.

As that class ended and we walked back to our homeroom class, Ms. Murphy, my homeroom teacher, kept sighing loudly. Though it appeared that I was still (hopefully?) the only one who realized I needed a bra, it was suddenly clear that I was not the only one who'd noticed my shoes squeaked. As we entered the classroom, Ms. Murphy snapped. She laid into me in front of the entire class about my squeaky shoes, of all things.

I was stunned. "I didn't do it on purpose," I stammered. That got me a notification slip for talking back. Maybe you're wondering what a notification slip is. I was, too, because I was a good kid and had no idea there were tiers to punishment when you were a "bad" kid.

A notification slip is a piece of white paper that details how you've misbehaved—in Ms. Murphy's crappy hand-writing. There's a space for a parent signature. If you get a notification slip, you don't get to watch the movie on Friday with the class, but rather you have to do some redundant chore like washing the chalkboard or sharpening pencils for hours until the bell rings at 1:45. I never saw any of the movies that year. One time I got close to seeing *Old Yeller*, but then I got in trouble for sneezing and was banished to eraser-cleaning duty.

Every week that I brought one home my mom was mad at me. She was mad at me a lot that year. I felt terrible add-ing disappointment to her plate after her mother had died. I thought I was responsible for my mom's happiness, and every week I failed. I didn't know it then, but I was quickly falling into a depression.

And it wasn't just sadness. My grades started to reflect it. The day I was handed my report card and had a C in social studies I cried. That's an understatement. I wailed. I blubbered. I rode the bus, sobbing. My stop, the elementary school my mother works at across town, was the last one.

I sat alone, paralyzed by the disappointment I was sure to inspire when she finally saw that I'd brought home the lowest grade I'd ever had on a report card up to this point. It was a C-minus. Not even just a C, but basically a D-plus. I'd had straight As up until now, but fifth grade was my first real brush with "not-good-enough-ness."

My eyes were almost swollen shut. My nose was running. My throat ached. I slowly walked through the school to her office and couldn't speak. She ran to me and held me to her chest.

"What, Kilah? What happened?" she asked. She must have assumed I'd seen a dead body and had been framed for murder.

She was disappointed, and since my mother's approval was all I had going for me anymore, I was shattered. I found comfort in food and sleeping, coming home after school and eating bowls of cereal and handfuls of chips and then lying down around eight p.m. to face the next day. I stopped believing I was smart. Perhaps it was an elaborate lie, a cruel trick that had set me up and everyone was laughing because I'd fallen for it. I'd have to find a new identity. *Akilah the High Achiever* was now retired. Who was I now?

Back at school, things were getting worse, not better. I still get enraged when I think about Black History Month that year. What was usually a joyous occasion of a big-butt TV being rolled in and the lights being dimmed was now tainted by racism by omission. Ms. Murphy took the VHS out of its cardboard and slid it into the VCR as the room lit up with that familiar blue light.

It was a video day. Video days were a rare treat. Typically Ms. Murphy gave some sort of introduction to the video we were about to watch, explaining how it was related to the overall lesson plan and wasn't just an excuse for us to goof off while she graded homework. But today Ms. Murphy hit play without an explanation of any kind. The video was footage of dogs biting young black people wearing their Sunday best. Powerful hoses knocked down elderly black people. Acid was poured into swimming pools. The ugliest things humanity was capable of was the cinematic selection for the afternoon . . . *Yay.* The other fifth graders (all of them were white) laughed. Hard. And who could blame them? Without a basic understanding of the fact that this was not fiction, not a slapstick comedy, and with hardly any concept of Martin Luther King being literally murdered soon after this footage was taken, it feels so fantastical as to not be real. My face felt hot. I hated everyone.

These kids were my *friends.* I'd played with them at recess, gushed about movies and books and TV shows with them. Ate lunch with them. Stayed at their houses, and they had no idea why I was crying. Why I felt singled out. Why this was the most painful public experience I'd gone through at that point in my young life.

I left the room, claiming I had to go to the bathroom (notification slip, getting up without raising my hand), and found a bathroom farther down the hall than the one right outside our class. I had to hide. I had to be alone and get it all out. Fifteen minutes or so of solace seemed fair, and I eventually came back to class, fixed my face, and pretended it was fine. After all, the only thing worse than watching white children laugh about the horrors and racism of the '60s is having to explain to them why they shouldn't laugh about the horrors and racism of the '60s. I was tired. It's an exhaustion that still lives in my bones today.

But finding that bathroom was a real sanctuary for me. Any time class got to be too much, I'd just go there. No one really knew about this restroom past the library. In fact, one of the stalls was just filled with books and boxes. A couple weeks after the Black History Month scandal, when I had diarrhea and wanted to use a bathroom away from the harsh judgment of my peers, I went to that restroom.

And that was the day Ms. Murphy took the one shred of dignity I had left. When I came out of the bathroom, she was standing there, towering menacingly, arms crossed, lipstick making its way onto multiple teeth.

"What are you doing down here?" she asked accusingly.

"I was using the bathroom," I said, hoping she hadn't heard the bubble-guts situation.

"That's a notification slip. If you want to play all day, then you can miss the movie." Heartless and unaware that I'd all but given up.

"Fine," I accepted.

"Fine? Well then, we need to have a parent-teacher conference!"

My "attitude" annoyed her. What she didn't know is that I *was* broken. The fact that I didn't care anymore was testament to that. She was enraged.

A few nights later, Ms. Murphy, my mom, and I sat at a table in the classroom. Ms. Murphy just told my mom how terrible I was forever, but I finally stood up for myself.

"She makes me read the slave narratives. All of them. Out loud. None of the white kids have to," I said, deciding if she was going to tell on me, I was going to tell on her.

"Excuse me, what?" my mom said right on cue. I've always loved my mother, but I loved her in that moment like I loved watching Mufasa scare away the hyenas on Simba's behalf.

Before Ms. Murphy could respond, I continued.

"She made us watch stuff about Martin Luther King like it was wrestling." *Ooh, bitch, you gon' get it now.* "And when everybody laughed she didn't even say that he was killed!"

I saw Ms. Murphy look scared for the first time in my life. My mom gets this primal, rage-filled look on her face when she's pissed. Her jaw clenches, her eyes squint ever so slightly behind her glasses. She seems to involuntarily shake her head. It was all coming. But then:

"Akilah was using the bathroom down the hall! I have no control over her," Ms. Murphy said, maybe admitting exactly what she wanted anyway.

"Why did you use the bathroom down the hall, Kilah?" my mom asked, totally losing the thread of us taking down Ms. Murphy together.

"Because I had DIARRHEA!" I said, furious.

And with that, my mother started laughing. It started out silently, more shoulders bouncing and hand over face than sound. But then it did become laughter, and I started laughing. Ms. Murphy knew better than to join us.

We stayed like this for a couple minutes, my mom wiping tears under her glasses. With a final "whew," my mom let her know what was up.

"We've been through a lot this year. My mother passed away last summer."

"I'm sorry." Ms. Murphy tried to get on her good side, but my mom knew better.

"So anyway, none of this seems to be that big of a deal. I don't like having to come down to the school for nonsense. Did she hurt anybody?"

"No."

"And she hasn't acted out?"

"Well, she went to that bath—"

"So then what is the problem? What is this really about?" My mom, my hero.

And that was that.

The next school year I had straight As again. We don't really talk about it much as a society, but the expectation that teachers have for us and our level of comfort in the classroom dictates a lot of our success and "aptitude." How can anyone be apt to do anything in a place where they feel not only underrepresented, but misrepresented and attacked?

In later years I learned to stand up for myself to teachers like Ms. Murphy. From kindergarten through twelfth grade I never had a black teacher. Not one. No one in power looked like me, save for a vice principal that I never encountered. It took that experience in fifth grade to learn not to suffer silently when I was being mistreated. It took seeing my mother handle this woman who I thought was untouchable without kid gloves.

And yes, I'll be using whatever bathroom I find, thanks.

Birthdays Are, Too

Every family has an established dynamic that finds its way after a number of years. Sure, there are the defined roles by birth order and personality traits, but there are also the ways you learn to survive one another's stronger features.

Birthday parties in my house were an ethnographic study into the minds of my family members.

My sister Lanie is a day short of a year older than me. That means my birthday is the day before hers a year later. It's the kind of mental math that looks fine on paper, but explaining it publicly was a lot harder than just telling everyone that, yes, we were twins. Because of our close birthdays, we had shared birthday parties throughout our formative years.

The point of birthday parties has always eluded me.

Sure, party hats and cake are fun, but why do I have to give you a gift for successfully evacuating your mother's body? She and the dedicated doctors at So-And-So Medical Center's pediatric wing deserve to be showered with gifts for the anniversary of your birth, not you. You probably looked like a sticky alien dough monster that first day anyway, so why's *that anniversary* worth celebrating?

If I *had* to have a party, though, I wanted it to be big. Not because I thought I *deserved* it, but because I liked attention. I wanted people to spend a day fawning over me while I put out a fire with my mouth. My favorite Polaroid picture ever is from Linzy Ball's third birthday party at our preschool. Both our mothers worked at the elementary school, and it was a cost-effective alternative to the standard Discovery Zone pizza-ball-pit-tokens-and-tickets fare. In the photo, I'm sitting at a table filled with smiling little boys and girls with fluffy bangs, arms folded neatly at my chest, sporting a face that has since been perfected by unimpressed Olympic gymnast McKayla Maroney.

"What's wrong, Kiwi?" Linzy's grandmother asked as she picked me up onto her lap.

"I want a party," I said coldly.

"You can have a party, sweetie." She tried and failed to convince me.

"I *already had* a birthday this year," I whined.

But the idea had been planted, and in a few years I would finally get my in-school birthday party. Little did I know that my obsession with my own birthday would erode each year until I'd eventually dread its arrival.

On my seventh birthday (Lanie's eighth), my mom decided to clear out a space in the largest hallway of the school for our extravaganza. There was pizza, cake, and a boom box in lieu of a DJ. All of our friends and all the kids whose parents were super late picking them up from school were prepared to have the kind of memorable, self-exploratory, immersive experience that Burning Man can *only attempt* to provide to its annual attendees.

Everything was going as planned, with all of us kids dancing around and playing whatever dumb games eight-year-olds make up, until Ashley Spiders took over.

Ashley, my (ex) best friend, was a major show-off. Her middle name was *literally* Star. Her hair was blonde and big, and her blue eyes sparkled. Besides looking like an actual doll, she was the loudest, most confident, most coordinated girl among us. Ashley competed and won pageants and was head cheerleader for the local peewee football team.

She always had the first party of the year because her birthday was the first week of January, which automatically

set the bar high for everyone else's shindigs. In addition
to the usual Chuck E. Cheese affair, her mom often rented
two hotel rooms at the Holiday Inn, where we'd swim, scarf
pizza, and commandeer the hot tub like a crew of six-year-
old pirates.

Being (ex) best friends with Ashley was a distinct
power position. I was likable enough, but I didn't possess
her celebrity it-factor that dictated the hierarchy on the
playground. With Ashley by my side, I always got first dibs
on four square.

The charm that had been my ticket to elementary
school popularity, however, completely rained out my seventh birthday party. That year, Quad City DJ's iconic hit
"C'Mon 'N Ride It (The Train)" came out, giving hordes of
uncoordinated children the confidence to hold on to one
another's shoulders in the shape of a conga line while the
conductor at the engine of the train got the distinct honor of
pumping their arms up and down like a maniac whose bus
driver just skipped their stop.

Can anyone tell me why Ashley took it upon herself to conduct the train? On this, my day of birth? Lanie
and I swiftly jumped off the train and stood in the corner,
seething. The nerve! The disrespect! We never showed up
to her parties at Chuck E. Cheese to steal her shine. We'd

just participate in the children's gambling disguised as Skee-Ball—seriously, why do we let kids spend tokens to play games that they can't win? Doesn't that seem like a mistake??? Ashley had effectively ruined our party. Still, we couldn't let our mom know how furious we were.

"She's *your* friend! Do something!" Lanie whined.

"The song is almost over. Maybe we can cool it on the dancing?" And a plan was born. Like many of our childhood shenanigans, I was deployed to plant an idea in my mom's head and have her think it was her own idea. This had worked at the library every time we wanted to rent the "Caldifoohnia Waisins" VHS tape even though we had just returned it. It worked when trying to lessen Lanie's time-out sentences for my own personal Barbie-playing gain. It would work again.

"Mommy. Can we play a game without music? I wanna play jump ropes," I whined so well that I even convinced myself that I wanted nothing more.

"Cut the music! We're gonna sing 'Happy Birthday'!" my mom announced to whoever was standing close to the stereo. Our happiness was now their distinct responsibility.

The music didn't return after the cake situation. Partially because my mom did not cheap out and bought way too much cake and we all ate too much cake. Too full to dance. But not too full to play Uno and Go Fish for another hour.

But honestly, none of this compares to the third-grade sleepover fiasco that was both legendary and the last time our mom ever let us do anything with friends at our house.

My mom had recently bought a new car, and Lanie and I stood in the doorway of our laundry room that led to the garage patiently awaiting her return. Once the five kids were there, it was a pretty regular birthday party; there was a ton of pizza. (Pizza in Kentucky sucks, but I wouldn't really find that out until I moved to NYC and tried real pizza for the first time. It turns out the secret ingredient is diversity.) Little white girls gave us a variety of black Barbie dolls. Well, two attendees gave us the same "Workin' Out Barbie" complete with lime-green spandex and a cassette tape with inspirational cardio music, but who's counting?

We choreographed a dance and ate too much and played games that centered on being in a sleeping bag and falling asleep first. No one fell asleep. We told jokes until Kaitlin peed her pants and had to change. We tried to tell ghost stories, but we didn't really know how to be scary yet, so we all gave up about halfway through the plot. We were definitely the popular girls at our party that year, Lanie and me. I think we brushed our teeth at least five times that night because each girl wanted to individually brush with us.

All was harmonious in our house until about three a.m., when my mom snapped.

"If y'all don't shut up and go to bed, I swear to God I'm taking your little asses home. I am *not* playin'!" she shouted down from her bedroom to the living room. Apparently the repeated screeches of our never-ending laughter were unsettling.

Lanie and I immediately understood the weight of this situation. Once Marilynn was mad it was only a few minutes before she would launch into her hour-long script about how we didn't appreciate her and we had to go to our rooms because *how many times did she tell us to stop?*

Unfortunately, our friend group had different kinds of parents at their own houses—probably vampires okay with being kept up in the middle of the night on a day of the week designed for sleeping in.

Try as we might, we just couldn't keep the other girls quiet. Much to Lanie's and my chagrin, the laughter continued, and an hour later another threat descended the stairs.

"Okay. Y'all wanna go home? No. NO! I told y'all to be

quiet. Go. To. Bed. If I hear one more peep, I'm driving you all home and your moms are going to be so pissed when I wake them up. Keep it up!" she dared us.

I eventually fell asleep, so I don't know if the standoff between giggles and my exhausted mom was continuing. I just know that at eight a.m. I was awoken by the sound of my mom pulling out of the driveway fast. I rolled over and shook Lanie awake. Our friends were gone. We were screwed.

I immediately suggested we clean up before Mom got back. After all, I was the peacekeeper in the home. My strategy was simply to anticipate what might make her mad after a sleepless night. I took stock of the litany of things that could be out of place. We put our pajamas in the hamper so she wouldn't have to see them. We cleaned the toilet and sinks. We vacuumed the snack crumbs and took all the pizza boxes to the trash.

Lanie and I waited patiently in the laundry room near the garage for her return this time. We were prepared to get yelled at for misbehaving for a whopping twelve hours straight. I came to terms with it, but Lanie was a nervous wreck.

"We're never going to have another sleepover!" she said, thinking the worst.

"Well, we never had one before now, so maybe we should be grateful for the memories . . ."

"I *tried* to tell them to be quiet! It was more your friends than my friends!" She bounced between all of the stages of grief.

"We have the same friends! Don't put this on me. This is not the same as Discovery Zone '95. This is more like that time you ate the block of cheese Mom was gonna use for mac and cheese last Thanksgiving."

The garage door opened slowly and we took a deep breath in unison. By this point in our young lives we had learned that it's better to take the yelling early in the day and get it over with.

Before Mom closed her car door she reached across to the front passenger seat to lift a box of doughnuts.

SCORE! Mom didn't even bring up the night before. I was her fourth and youngest child; she knew that kids would be kids and sometimes that is in direct conflict with adult ideas of control and relaxation. She *let it go*. Lanie was shocked, but I have always been a little better at going with the flow. And sometimes the flow led to doughnuts.

I Don't Love Animals

Like every other thing in my life, our family pets weren't normal. Couldn't we just be like the Tanners from *Full House* and have a golden retriever? Nope. Mom was allergic to dogs *and* cats. Could we do a light quirky thing with a bird? Absolutely not. There was "too much noise" in the house already. Instead we had a house of horrors: a bizarre motley crew of mammals, crustaceans, and whatever classification fish are. Again, *not normal*.

In the year 2000, my Christmas list wasn't too extensive. I mostly just wanted a turtle, because I'd read in school that they're self-sufficient and far more entertaining than the fish I'd amassed and somehow not killed in four years. Yes, my fish survived the rise and fall of the

Spice Girls. In second grade my class had two pet turtles, and aside from smelling a tad rank as we approached summer, they required very little attention. Plus, we had a backyard so we could just put their tank out there when the funk got too real. *This* was a pet experience my family could get behind.

On Christmas Eve, my mother inexplicably came home with a rabbit in a cage.

"Turtles have salmonella, Kilah. I'm not tryna die in here," she said. I was at once delighted and horrified. I wasn't ready to take off my pet-ownership training wheels, and a rabbit required a level of physical contact that I wasn't prepared to explore. *Petting?* What the hell is that? I "liked" animals; I just didn't want them touching me. Still, the bunny was cute and tiny, and I was ten so basically all I cared about were cute and tiny things.

Lanie loved animals and rushed to take our new black-and-white dwarf bunny out of its cage to hold carefully in her lap. I was the Cruella de Vil to her Jack Hanna, only comfortable around animals when eating or wearing them. While she softly caressed our new fuzzy son, we tried to come up with a really good name for him.

"Eve?" Lanie posited, listing the date of arrival as the obvious reason such a name would be fitting.

"No," Mom said. "Y'all aren't going to annoy me screaming 'Eve' all the time in the house."

Lanie's next attempt: "Juno?" With no improv training,
the frozen tundra that Kentucky had transformed into
during the recent snowfall meant that the capital of Alaska
was her best word association. In hindsight, had we pre-
empted the hit Ellen Page movie and actually named the
bunny Juno, we would have so much Brooklyn/Portland
cred now. *sigh*

"Hmm . . . nope," Mom replied.

"Bunbun?" I added mindlessly. I was hardly paying
attention to anything but the rabbit's constantly wiggling
nose and long eyelashes. What was he thinking about?
Was he missing the pet store? Did he understand that this
was a permanent change? Was he gonna bite Lanie? He
seemed benign enough, but I still wasn't ready to investigate
closer.

"YES!" Mom and Lanie said in unison. We'd done
it. Bunbun was an official member of the family. It was a
Christmas miracle.

Instinctively I grabbed the tube of rabbit chow and
poured some into the bowl as Lanie lowered Bunbun back
into his cage. Insanely diminutive, Bunbun hopped into the
bowl to feast. After about ten minutes of nonstop chewing,

we realized that history could and would repeat itself[1] if we didn't intervene and remove the food from Bunbun's cage.

Bo came home a while later, and we met him at the door to introduce him to the family's latest addition.

"His name's Bunbun," I announced, thinking it more clever than when it was simply an afterthought.

"Nah, let's call him Li'l Turk," he suggested, after his most recent rap obsession.

Bo was then, and still is now, the most elusive member of my family. Five years older than me, we never had much in common. I definitely thought he was the coolest, and he definitely thought I was the perfect target for Nerf darts and balls. If he wasn't shooting me, he was closing his bedroom door on me to listen to Master P or call one of the endless high school girls that had a crush on him.

"No! BO! COME ON! Say hi to Bunbun!" Lanie couldn't control herself and picked Bunbun up out of the cage for Bo to hold.

---

1 We'd lost many fish to overfeeding thanks to the *Adventures of Mary-Kate & Ashley* VHS tapes that showed them feeding their fish before embarking on every adventure. In hindsight, we should have never been trusted with feeding fish the right amount when none of us was even feeding ourselves the right amount of food. Piles of Doritos would have been a fitting sponsor of my childhood.

Bunbun scratched and kicked and Bo lost his grip and dropped Bunbun in the cage roughly.

"Fuck that." And with that, Bo went up to his room to listen to his music loudly. Teenagers.

Maybe his name wasn't unanimous, but his main points of contact would continue to call him Bunbun for the duration of his time on earth.

Rabbits were way different than we expected. Their nails get so long and they scratch the shit out of you. Lanie and I *still* have scars fifteen years later. They also pee and shit everywhere. Then they get bored and start eating their own shit. It's gross. Why do they eat their own butt poop? Whose idea was that? And what's worse, sometimes they eat their crap and then try to lick you with their crap-tongue and then BAM! There's *another* memory you're going to have to push away when you're lying awake in the late hours of night decades later.

My oldest sister Tasha's then-boyfriend, Chris, came over once and we decided to let him hold Bunbun. We thought Chris was the coolest, so we really wanted them to hit it off. Tasha watched us intently, waiting to find out what way we'd embarrass her this time. The last time she had to babysit us during a date to see *The Lost World: Jurassic Park*, I cried during the scene where the guy gets eaten through the waterfall and the water runs red—loud enough to get us all kicked out. It was not a distant enough memory for there to be any slipups this time.

Bunbun wasn't quite as enamored with Chris as any of us were and proceeded to pee all over him and his white tee.

One time Bunbun got loose in the morning and was way too fast for any of us to catch him.

"He's going under the couch!" I screamed as he made a hard right out of the living room.

"Secure the perimeter!" Lanie yelled as Mom and I put up couch cushions to make sure there was only one way in and one way out.

Bunbun ran right into our trap, but then climbed up my mom's shoulder, parkoured onto the couch cushions that had collapsed without a couch behind them, and exited again, leaving us looking like Elmer Fudd's dumb ass trying to catch Bugs.

Regrouping, we decided to try a new strategy. Clearly we'd have to corner him in the moment. Just then, Bunbun came flying over the couch cushions back into the room.

"Ahhh!"

"Is somebody throwing him?"

We knocked over tables and threw shoes around trying to find and capture him.

"Grab him already!" I yelled, exasperated at Lanie. Bunbun's cage was in her room, and she would always take him out in the morning, risking it all for a little bit of love from him.

"I'm trying," she yelled back, missing him as he bee-lined under another chair.

"I'm on my way. The rabbit got loose again, so I'll just keep you posted," my mom explained to work, laughing, and hung up.

After two hours of unabated chaos, the whole down-stairs looked like that scene in *Kill Bill* after Uma Thurman's character, Black Mamba, breaks everything in the living room and kitchen and then shoots Vivica A. Fox's character, Copperhead, through the cereal box and tries to convince her victim's now-orphan daughter that her puppy caused all of the destruction. We eventually cornered Bunbun between two pillows and a plant and got him back in the cage. Since it was now noon, Mom let us stay home from school for the remainder of the day.

Aside from a few funny, formative episodes with him,[2] Bunbun was a *hassle*. He learned how to escape from the

2   Ricky Martin's since-forgotten song "Shake Your Bon-Bon" was blow-ing up the charts, and we'd hold Bunbun's front paws, change the words to fit his name, and dance around every single time it came on the radio like

cage, and we'd often come home to him roaming around eating poisonous houseplants. He had intermittent seizures that caused him to have explosive diarrhea on everything we owned.

The last straw was when Bunbun started screaming in the night. And I mean *screaming*. No one talks about it, but rabbits scream like people. It's high-pitched and jarring, like Taylor Swift on helium. None of us was expecting it, so the first time it happened my mom came running down the hall with her revolver screaming, "WHO'S IN HERE? WHO'S IN HERE?!" and Lanie had to talk her down and explain that something was wrong with Bunbun. This happened every night during the best part of every dream for *months*.

One day we came home and Bunbun was rock-hard and cold. I wrongly assumed he had picked up some new annoying habit that we'd have to correct. Nope. He'd died—presumably from the blunt-force trauma of trying to break out of the cage on which we'd started putting stacks of weighty books to stop his daily reenactments of *Escape from Alcatraz*.

"Good riddance. He smelled awful anyway," my mom

---

any of your favorite '90s feel-good family films. Or that time Bunbun was aggressively humping my calf and I had no idea what was happening and was screaming at my mom to stop the madness but she couldn't stop laughing.

said as she coldly put his stiff body in a garbage bag. Her touching eulogy continued as she dug a hole in the backyard, remembering to lament how chewed up everything had gotten and how thankful she was knowing her food would have fewer clumps of rabbit hair tainting it in the future. After trashing the rest of the cage, Mom handed Lanie and me the plastic clamps that attached the metal bars of the cage to its plastic bottom to remember him by. My life returned to normal pretty quickly, but Lanie *still* misses Bunbun and has acquired numerous dogs, rats, rabbits, and birds since his death to fill the bunny-shaped hole in her heart.

High school was a largely pet-less time in our lives (save for the few fish that wouldn't be cool for *once* and just die already). Life was moving along great until one summer when a peculiar nightly scratching sound started haunting our house.

Was it a rat? Was it a serial killer? Was it a ghost? We had no idea, but it scratched above every bedroom after ten p.m. every night. One night my mom called me up to her room because there was a raccoon staring at her from behind the screen in her bathroom window and she needed a witness. The culprit had been found.

For *years* my mother took to literally barking like a dog

and shooting Nerf guns at the ceiling to scare the raccoons out of the house. It never once worked but remained hilarious regardless.

The summer of 2005 was a truly strange time in my life. I had begun working at Hershey's Ice Cream in the old mall food court with a bunch of self-described "emo kids." We all got along because their sadness meant I never had to ask how they were doing. It also meant that I was introduced to a slew of bands on Myspace.com that reminded me that no matter how well-adjusted and understood I felt, how could that be possible if I was a teenager? We all decided to take our feelings to Warped Tour in lieu of opening shop one July day, and what was the hottest day of my life became literally hellish. I bought a room-temp Powerade and tried to down a chicken quesadilla from Taco Bell to soothe my headache, but heat exhaustion had set in. I got home, smelled something heinous, vomited all over the bathroom, and then slept on my cool sheets for six hours.

Only later did I find out that the ghastly, vom-inducing smell was baby raccoon carcasses that had rotted in the walls. That's right. The big-ass raccoon from the window that night had idiotically laid babies IN THE WALL. And they died! *Because they're babies.*

* * *

Summers later, when Lanie and I were both home from college, a truly crazy thing would happen: the raccoons would get all the way in the house.

I've always preferred a bedtime schedule more closely associated with babies and grandmas, and even as a teen I liked being in bed before ten. This particular summer night I had tucked in early. Around eleven p.m., Lanie started screaming.

"IT'S IN HERE! It's in here!!!!" she screamed from the kitchen directly under my bedroom.

Down the hall from me, Mom opened her door and started screaming, "WHAT?! WHAT'S IN HERE?!" and simultaneously watched a raccoon come up the stairs and go through the cracked door into Bo's defunct bedroom.

That's when the texting started.

Mom: It's in here! IT'S IN HERE!

Me: I heard! What are we going to do? Will it kill us???

Mom: We have to leave the house. FUCK THE HOUSE!

Homelessness had to be better than being eaten alive by vermin. I would have to put on pants and pack a suitcase and unlock my door and go downstairs to flee. We'd reconvene at mom's RAV4 and head for shelter at Tasha's house. By this point in my life, Tasha had finished both college and law school and was living a pretty swanky life about ten miles north of us in her own house. Chic and adult, there was always a fear that we'd break something. Even though we were fully teenagers and not complete idiots.

Frozen solid, I lay there and contemplated the alternative: if the raccoons could tunnel in, it would only be a matter of time before I would wake up to one chewing on my eyebrows.

That settled it. I quietly turned on a lamp and got out of bed, scared that maybe another raccoon was under my bed and would try to bite my ankle. It was irrational, but all bets are off when you have to defend your home from fuzzy intruders.

I quietly picked out the essentials. Underwear. A pile of shirts, shorts, and jeans. My two decent bras. I began to open my bedroom door when I heard my mother scream.

"What?! Oh god, what?" I yelled back.

"Nothing, you scared me with your door! Hurry up!"

My heart was now beating in my ears. I crossed the hall into the bathroom and shut the door behind me. I grabbed an amalgam of toothbrushes, toothpastes, and face washes. If I needed anything else, we'd just have to make a Kroger run tomorrow.

Just then there was a knock on the bathroom door.

"Ah!" I screamed.

"Quit yellin'! It's just me!" my mom shouted. "I'm head-ing down, are you ready?"

I zipped my suitcase and cracked the door. We looked at each other. I guess I thought she was going to count down from three or something, but there was no time. With the stealthiness of Seal Team Six we descended the stairs and fled to the car, looking back at our home for probably not the last time, but we weren't sure.

We all fled. I was kind of excited to be staying at Tasha's house for two weeks while my mom's weird rugged friend set traps of antifreeze and rat poison and peanut butter, hoping that something would kill them, but nothing ever did. The moment we thought they were gone for good, a new one would be back, knocking like Poe's goddamn raven forevermore. When we finally moved back in we all just agreed not to open Bo's bedroom door. He had found an apartment with his girlfriend and had no real attachment to the stuff in his room anymore anyway.

A couple months later we moved. We didn't even bother going into Bo's room to fix it up. It wasn't worth it. Whatever sucker would move there after us would just have to deal with the generational raccoon war. We were tapping out.

Still, if I'm in Kentucky and we're driving at night and we see a raccoon, let's just say none of us is swerving to miss it.

These days, my most common encounters with wildlife happen at bodegas late at night or on the subway. The rats stay in their lane (on the tracks) and bodega cats know to get out of the way when I'm ordering my one a.m. bacon, egg, and cheese on a roll, three napkins, *please*. I wish my heart was big enough to love all the animals in the animal kingdom, but I'm content to just smile at pups at the dog park from a safe distance or let my friend's cats walk across my lap while we're watching Netflix.

But seriously, fuck raccoons.

Internet Person

I don't remember the first time I got on the internet. It must have happened sometime between playing Oregon Trail (a game where children try to ford a river and shoot squirrels and not die of cholera on a treacherous journey across the country) and designing my first Geocities page, which was literally just a quiz asking visitors (of which there were maybe five over the course of its lifespan) what their favorite pizza-flavored snack was. Unsurprisingly it was pizza rolls. I absolutely do remember a time before the internet, but I don't think I ever felt truly myself before the internet.

I spent a lot of time in extracurricular activities. And my mom spent a lot of time waiting in the car for me to be finished with them. Too much time, probably. Years later

I'd talk with my therapist about how over-socialization has made me far too well-adjusted and really good at hiding my own problems from other people and also myself. Anyway.

Upon entering the fourth grade, I became the newest member of Latonia Elementary School's "webbies" team. It was more of a club than a team, since none of us was in shape and the entire "sport" took place in desk chairs in front of those bulbous, colorful iMacs in our computer lab. Still, having lightly supervised internet time was like what it must have felt like to be the kid from *Blank Check*. The movie is pretty self-explanatory. A kid gets a blank check and then just buys everything including a mansion with a secret waterslide exit.

Three times a week after school I'd arrive at the computer lab, sit down, type in my username and password (predetermined by the school to keep us behaving), and open the Paint program. Paint was basically the caveman version of Instagram except there were no feeds or stories, but it was absolutely a way to waste time by looking at something pretty. I'd pick the paint can, choose the color "rainbow," and click on the blank canvas, prepared to type something stupid like "Akilah RULES!" in fluorescent green and then beg the teacher to let me print it out, using half the computer lab's colored ink in the process.

Why I needed this printed out, I don't know. Then, I'd click Netscape. I almost feel bad comparing it to Google Chrome, because it was *just* a browser, but a really really really crappy one. Imagine waiting two-ish minutes for the homepage to load, and then, since there was no social media, typing in whatever was on your mind: *Beanie Babies. Britney Spears. Butterfly hair clips.* I'd scroll incredibly slowly as the images loaded one at a time like when you have to squeeze the shampoo bottle for just a little spittle of product to dot your hand over and over before you get frustrated and decide that smelling like a hot scalp is not the worst thing one can smell like. At the same time I was seeing roughly four images and web pages over the course of a very slow hour, my mom was exploring the internet for the first time herself.

"I'm a webMASTER, Kilah!" my mom exclaimed proudly. She had started taking a Saturday "webmaster" class. Usually Saturdays were reserved for HGTV-inspired Lowe's runs or something else time-consuming like hypnotism or yelling at us for not cleaning the house.

"MASTER" was a loose term (a few months into webbies I would teach her how to copy and paste, changing the trajectory of her afternoons forever), but she was super on board with my newfound obsession with computers. Webbies was basically one free hour after school during which we would learn a few HTML tricks to build the school's website (complete with unlicensed cardinal images from the Ask Jeeves search engine). It got me out of my mom's hair, and she was able to catch up on the latest Janet Evanovich book without being bothered.

But it was here, in the afternoons between three and four p.m. in an elementary school computer lab, where I got hooked on the social media gateway drug: Neopets. Neopets was an entire universe. The site had every kind of environment. There was a desert, a jungle, a tundra. Once logged in you got a free fictional pet and through games and events could earn enough points to buy a paintbrush (to make your unicorn-ass creature look like the night sky or a rainbow or flames). You could even save enough points to eventually buy special snacks for your pet, or even buy more pets. I believe Webkinz is the modern equivalent, but do I look like the kind of person who is going to type "Webkinz" into the search bar to be sure?

I have a theory that every person you love online who has mastered the balance of self-deprecating oversharing and well-adjusted cool got indoctrinated on Neopets. Don't believe me? I have receipts.

Chrissy Teigen tweeted a thread about Neopets while she was pregnant, and we *all* love her:

"I miss Neopets.

"I was a comment board moderator. I won multiple caption contests. I've basically been told to barely move and let my baby grow so fuck it, I'm going back on neopets.

"oh my god neopets has not changed a bit. the omelette . . . is still cooking"

Mara Wilson (who has an impeccable Twitter feed and performed a voice on one of my favorite shows, *BoJack Horseman*) once tweeted:

"Where are the nostalgic Neopets think pieces? Where are they?"

Neopets had everything. Sci-fi creatures that were both inventive and cute, chat rooms where we all role-played and wrote bizarre fan fiction about literally anybody, but mostly the Hanson brothers. The site also had games. An omelet every season where you could get a snack for ya pets or a cave where you could get a paintbrush to paint your Tuskaninny. Good times.

Mind you, this was pre–social media, so any and all friends you made here must really like what you were posting. Hate-following wasn't a thing yet, and everyone was earnestly trying to raise their Neopets to be productive members of Neopian society. This website truly was where many of us learned how to exist online with strangers, make them our friends, and tell stories that were compelling enough to keep us using our brain cells after school.

It was also the portal to a world where I could be whoever I wanted to be. Back then you didn't want anyone to know where you were anywhere at any time. Heaven forbid you were home when someone you didn't know rang your doorbell. Every stranger was a potential kidnapper. Now we order strangers to pick us up in their Toyota Camrys and tell them exactly where we will be in the event that they actually drop us off and don't gut us like fish. I quickly created an alter ego: Zoe Maloney. She was an average-height white girl with red hair and green eyes (the description I'd give in the Neopets chat rooms). She was on the cheerleading squad (because I wasn't) but never made a big deal about it (although *sometimes* she would wear her uniform to school). Oh, and she had every flavor of Lip Smackers because of her generational wealth. Before you jump down my throat, *yes*, I pretended to be a white ten-year-old online when I was a black ten-year-old. In my defense: Beyoncé had not yet been introduced into pop culture, and I went to a school with a bunch of white kids who were actively learning to judge me because their parents judged black people. It was exhausting. So yes, before I let myself be invited and then uninvited to a sleepover (because Cassie's mom was uncomfortable with having a ten-year-old black girl in her house), in the chat room, I decided that it was easier to be anyone else online because it felt easier to be anyone else in the real world.

The ritual of sitting down at a computer and just searching for whatever I could think of was the best way to pass the time. Nostalgia started before puberty for my generation—digging through our memories to find toys from our childhood, commercials we remembered being funny, and getting to relive every canceled show, forgotten book, and moment whenever we wanted. None of us was really considered all that cool, but we were certainly before our time in terms of wasting time on the internet.

AOL instant messenger ushered in more reasons to commandeer the phone line. Why would I talk to these kids on the phone when I could type, like, ten words a minute with my tiny ten-year-old hands?

In *The Lion King*, Simba's adolescence is portrayed as him walking across an endless log with Timon and Pumbaa. Well, my puberty log was dial-up internet and LiveJournal (archaic Tumblr), and instead of us singing "Hakuna Matata," I just listened to that really obnoxious AOL CD's fax machine–esque sound. I think most millennials relate.

I am now a fully formed internet person, and that's far more accepted now than it was when I was a little kid. Is it woefully misunderstood still? Yes. But those early days were the genesis of my story. Talking to strangers online and investigating Neopia and writing fan fiction for other kids informed how cool people would think I was online later, when I could look back fondly at how small the internet was. We built entire societies with other people, while other people were finishing their homework and watching TV. We should give Neopets, Zoog Disney, and all the weirdos therein the credit they deserve. Twitter, Facebook, and the internet as we know it now would not exist if not for the geniuses who taught us how to be people online. The internet was a subculture, and sometimes I mourn that loss, but it's now for everyone, and everyone is better for those who spent all of their free time knowing the internet could be more than just a solo experience.

Racism to a Fifteen-Year-Old Girl

I've had a recurring dream my whole life about being shot in the back.

The news media talks about race like it's the annual flu vaccine or poll results after an election. They talk about figureheads who are long dead or long gray, speaking about "progress" and "the mountaintop" and "the dream." They add numerical statistics like "Black people are thirty-one times as likely to be gunned down by police as white people" or "Black people are seven times less likely to be armed when shot by police than white people." They speak in numbers instead of families, friends—people. They talk about race like it is an abstract occurrence that might happen to other people, but certainly isn't happening to them. How can we solve the race problem? Is there a race problem? What race problem?

Racism is different to a fifteen-year-old girl.

Racism to a fifteen-year-old-girl is being told she's pretty for a black girl, as if she is pretty in spite of her beautiful grandmother, aunts, and mother.

Racism to a fifteen-year-old girl is reading "classic" literature that's classically racist with more than thirty incidents of the word "nigger" on a page, and being asked by her teacher why she's uncomfortable—effectively making the other twenty-four white students in class uncomfortable.

Racism to a fifteen-year-old girl is being told by her white classmate that she is whiter than him because of her less-stereotypical interests, regardless of the fact that she is the only black person he has ever met and had the nerve to speak to.

Racism to a fifteen-year-old girl is a river of white tears about Anne Frank's diary and the horrors of the Holocaust juxtaposed with rolling eyes, disdain, and exasperation at the mention of American slavery.

Racism to a fifteen-year-old-girl is being mocked for having short relaxed hair when her naturally long curly hair was too "kinky" and "coarse" to be lovable, either.

Racism to a fifteen-year-old girl is sitting on a bus while

the boys list all the most beautiful women in the world and realizing they are all white women.

Racism to a fifteen-year-old girl is the pin-dropping silence from her classmates turned strangers at the mention of Black History Month.

Racism to a fifteen-year-old girl is being shamed out of wearing her hair in braids by kids who call her "Kris Kross" while they simultaneously "ooh!" and "ahh!" over her white classmate's cornrow souvenir from her spring break trip to Jamaica.

Racism to a fifteen-year-old girl is a friend proclaiming that she can go to the "hood," but only if she'll accompany her because she's "scary enough to protect her."

Racism to a fifteen-year-old girl is crying at night because her crush thinks her nose and lips are too big—and he doesn't know why he thinks that, so he assumes it's not a societally influenced impulse, but rather an objective predilection.

Racism to a fifteen-year-old girl is being called scary because her skin doesn't burn in the sun.

Racism to a fifteen-year-old girl is a football player proclaiming proudly in a social studies class debate that he doesn't see race—something she literally has to live and breathe every single moment of her life.

Racism to a fifteen-year-old girl is worrying about the rise of gun violence in America, and fearing that if it ever happens at her school, she'd definitely be on the hit list—not because she's a bully, but because unwarranted hate toward her appearance goes unchecked.

Racism to a fifteen-year-old girl is hearing "I'm tired of talking about race" when it is twice as exhausting living it, as if she derives some secret pleasure in talking about the devastating effects of diaspora.

Racism to a fifteen-year-old girl is going to every dance alone, because none of her friends' white parents will consent to their children formally attending anything with a black girl and there aren't any other black kids at her school.

Racism to a fifteen-year-old girl is real. It is pervasive and ugly. It is the constant threat of depression, anxiety, and self-loathing.

And racism to a fifteen-year-old girl is wishing everyone you knew would understand that. It's wishing that you could survive the pimples and the braces and the crushes and the social hierarchy without the added burden of having to be aware of your skin color and how it makes *other people* feel all the time.

Best Friendship

Mindy Kaling tapped into something so true when she said, "Best friend isn't a person, it's a tier." Throughout the years I've had many best friends, and one ride-or-die forever best friend that I hope to die on the same day as because I can't fathom facing this world without her, even for a day. Plus I'd want her opinion on my funeral and vice versa. It would be a whole-ass mess without her. But sometimes you meet people who are acquaintances in best friend clothing.

Tiffany introduced herself to me by shoving me down on the playground in fourth grade. I like to run my mouth, even now, and I had apparently said too loudly that *her* best friend, Liz, had failed to look like Zenon: Girl of the 21st Century with her half-up pigtails, half-down hairdo. I was right, but that wasn't the point. Tiffany is loyal to a fault and had decided to stick up for her friend.

We were in different classes, so I didn't really run into her the rest of the year. Maybe we rode the same bus on our field trip to the state capital or the zoo, but it would require the passing of a few seasons for me to be reunited with this lanky white girl with full lips and freckles.

I've mentioned before that my elementary school was toilet white, so it shouldn't surprise you that Tiffany and I became friends when I stuck up for her after Teisa made fun of her lips (of all things) before social studies class.

"They're DSLs!" Teisa teased.

Teisa was on the cheerleading squad and had fiery red hair, freckles, braces, and no discernable upper lip. You remember that girl in elementary school that took gymnastics and would constantly be showing everyone how flexible she was by doing backbends, splits, and cartwheels like the lunch hour was a talent show? That was Teisa.

"What are those?" I asked.

"Dick-sucking lips!" she roared, and her friends with varying degrees of perversion laughed at this assertion. "And you have them, too!"

"Huh. Well, I suppose those kinds of lips are better than no lips at all. When you drink Kool-Aid does it just go everywhere?" I mimed a person desperately trying and failing to keep the sugar water inside their mouth.

"Bitch." Teisa pouted. Happy to have lightened the mood, I continued slurping and mocking her until I got a notification sheet for presumably having too hilarious a stand-up special.

From then on, Tiffany and I suffered the injustice of childhood and adolescence together.

Every night we'd talk on the phone for roughly an hour. That was the amount of time it took me to do a speed-run of Sonic CD on the old family PC and for Tiffany to get in trouble for not doing any number of chores and get kicked off the phone. The topics started with her crush, Chase, another gawky, tall white kid who wasn't in the "gifted" program. We were never superior about having been placed in the "smart kid classes," but we were curious about what the kids who weren't got to do instead of French class. After a half hour of musing, we'd talk about our celebrity crushes (since I had already decided all the boys I'd met were totally too boring to talk to for more than a minute). Hers was N*SYNC (Justin Timberlake was *so* cute and his favorite color was baby blue, too), and mine was Backstreet Boys (AJ had a bad-boy appeal that I was beginning to lean into). Sometimes there'd be lulls in conversation for minutes and minutes at a time while we both listened to the radio, separately but together. One such time a wedding classic, "Let's Get Married" by Jagged Edge, played to our captivated silence. It was the remix, and once the magnanimous rap line "WHAT'S GOING ON ACROSS THE SEAS" came in we were both rapping through the entire verse. It became known as our song™. We promised each other we would rap it at each other's weddings.

I liked Tiffany because she was always the most open-minded person in the room. When we argued it wouldn't last long because she was always willing to see multiple sides and then make a rational call, one that encouraged agreement. She also knew all the black people songs and all the white people songs. As much as she loved pop groups, she also knew the latest dance moves and R & B songs. I never had to worry about if she'd fit in with my family. She'd fit in with anybody.

The friendship quickly moved into sleepover territory. My mom hates when people come over with any amount of warning. If you spring people on her, she typically laments how "dirty our house is" for the better part of an hour and then enjoys the new person and getting a break from entertaining us. So, I was the first houseguest.

Standing on Tiffany's doorstep, my mom called to Tiffany's mom, Renee, from the car.

"She brought her own pillow case 'cause she has some

hair grease that might get on your pillows! She knows the phone number. I'll be back tomorrow afternoon!" And with that newfound freedom she peeled off.

Tiffany's house was small but nice. I put my stuff on the top bunk and turned around to see a man whose head nearly touched the ceiling lumbering through the room.

"Hey," her dad, Rob, mumbled as he made his way to the kitchen to hang with Tiffany's mom and little sister, Ashley.

After descending the bed frame's ladder, Tiffany presented me with options of what we could do.

"I have a PS2 and Crash Bandicoot," she offered. And we ate an icebox cake and played for hours until her parents got sick of us laughing. It felt good to know that all parents tire of children's laughter after a few too many hours.

The next morning her parents made a full breakfast of bacon, sausage, goetta, biscuits and gravy, and eggs *over medium*. I'd never had *over-medium* eggs. My mom doesn't like any food that isn't well-done. She believes foodborne illness is a real threat against which we should remain vigilant.

In addition to being in the talent show with a barely choreographed number to "5, 6, 7, 8" by Steps (one the many events I'm glad occurred in my life PRIOR to the boom of social media), she was my partner for all class projects. In sixth grade we made a trifold cardboard presentation about how marijuana was bad (it was a different time) and recorded a theme song to the rhythm of "The Lollipop Guild" song from *The Wizard of Oz.*

> *We represent*
> *The non-potheads*
> *The non-potheads*
> *The non-potheads*
> *And in the name of*
> *The non-potheads*
> *We wish you would abstain*
> *From smoking weed.*

I like to believe we got at *least* a B-plus.

When I skipped two grades and then transferred to public school, we still remained close. Since no one wanted to take me to the homecoming dance, I invited Tiffany. Since Kentucky is so small, kids from other schools coming to your dance was always a big deal.

Tiffany danced with everybody, and lo and behold all the boys who ignored me routinely were dancing back. I had a crush on Mr. Raney, a "permanent substitute" who was filling in for a math teacher on maternity leave, but wasn't so unrealistic as to believe we would ever date (come on).

Still, I suggested we stalk him around the dance, keeping a healthy distance but giving me enough information to write a diary entry about it the next day.

"No! I'm dancing!" Tiffany protested

"Come on! These guys are so boring!" I whined. But unfortunately, our stalking wouldn't work anyway. See, the guys liked Tiffany so much that even as we tried to perch near the cookies and punch table, all the guys followed us there, instantly blowing our cover.

"Hi, Mr. Raney," I said sheepishly.

"Hey, Akilah! Are you having a good time?" I was forever in the student zone. I knew this, but the heart wants what it wants. And the sadness I felt as he definitely went to go talk to other teachers (the most boring!) over me was a devastating blow. I tried to have a good time, but how could I? One day I'd have to grow into my own cuteness and find a boy my own age who liked me.

Our friendship was unshaken even as Tiffany entered high school. There'd be more dances and musicals and reasons for us to check out what was happening at the other's school. We rated the hotness of different boys by looking through old yearbooks.[3] Tiffany made another best friend

---

3 Do they still make yearbooks? What would be the point? You follow everyone you know on Instagram and then eventually you are Facebook friends fighting about politics and wondering why you even know them still

at her school, Emily, and I made one at my school, Stacy. I immediately liked Emily. She was quiet and maybe a bit too Jesus-y for my taste. But I can handle Bible-thumping. Tiffany did not like Stacy. Not even a little.

Stacy was also tall and white, but with jet-black hair and green eyes that she covered with blue contacts every day. One afternoon while I was wasting time pretending to take photos for "yearbook class," I noticed her in the special needs classroom. She was strikingly beautiful and sitting alone at a desk, appearing to take a test. I have no idea why I noticed her, but when she got on the bus for speech and drama at 4:30 a.m. one Saturday a few weeks later, I remembered.

"She is SO HOT," Isaac said. All the boys were beside themselves.

"Oh yeah, is she on the team now? I saw her in the special needs classroom the other week when I was taking pictures." It was so early that it hadn't occurred to me that this information might affect the way the guys saw her.

"She's like *retarded hot*," Isaac deadpanned idiotically. I listened to them reduce her to all of her "best" body parts until I couldn't take it anymore and went and sat by her.

and deciding to only go on the site on your birthday to say thanks for the birthday wishes in a vague status update that lets everyone know you're still alive but also not there for anything more than that.

"Hey, I'm Akilah. Don't look but all the junior guys are staring at you."

She turned her head to glance and they ducked behind the tattered leather seats.

"I'm Stacy. I just started as a freshman at Boone."

"Oh yeah? I saw you in the special needs room and didn't know if . . ."

"I was just taking a make-up exam. Did you tell everyone you saw me in there?" She blushed.

And I just had to laugh. But she laughed, too, and we drove the boys crazy all year.

In all honesty, this is what I liked about my friendship with Stacy. I finally got to be cool and fawned over. If a boy wanted a chance with Stacy he'd have to be nice to me, too. And Stacy really trusted me. I was often the third wheel that would put her parents at ease when she wanted to go on a proper date. If there was a video montage of my junior year of high school, it would be set to "You Make My Dreams" by Hall & Oates, and it would be footage of Stacy and her boyfriend holding hands at the skating rink, the bowling alley, and on her couch, and pan to the left or right to see me, just happy to be there.

Sleeping over at Stacy's house was different. Her

parents lived in a big subdivision and were constantly updating and renovating. The living room had surround sound embedded. Her parents' office had a newer, sleeker computer on a monthly basis. She had a projector screen in her basement where we'd play Guitar Hero or watch a movie I couldn't believe she hadn't seen yet, like *Back to the Future* or *Armageddon*.

I could never figure out why she hadn't seen stuff that had been out forever. Her family moved to Kentucky from California, and so it was put to me that kids out west didn't watch as much TV. I pitied them. But it wasn't just movies she didn't know about. One time we were in her room listening to the Alien Ant Farm version of "Smooth Criminal," and she didn't know Michael Jackson sang it first. I had to believe that maybe *she* was from an alien ant farm because who doesn't know every Michael Jackson hit? There's just no excuse for that level of ignorance.

Every time I spent the night her room had changed. It was either a different color, from red to teal to dark gray back to white, or it was literally a different room because she wanted to switch with her brother on a whim, and/or she had some new hobby her parents had invested in. The first time I came over she had this guitar she would play and sing songs by the Scorpions and AC/DC for me. The next time she had a pet snake she had to feed a rat to satiate it before bed. I could never keep up with who she was. One day she was decked out in clothes from Hot Topic, the next she was deep in the preppy styles from Hollister. All the while I was wearing a few name-brand clothes, but mostly whatever was the second-to-worst thing at Walmart and Old Navy.

The only constant in my sleeping over was that her family could not cook and never would. We'd eat cereal or butter on noodles. If they ordered a pizza, there were never toppings.

"I don't like sauce," Stacy would complain. I still don't relate on a human level to hating all sauces. Like, what?

There was also this bizarre weekend ritual where her mom would wake us up in the morning. On a Saturday. Before ten a.m. When Tiffany would come to my house, my mom absolutely would *not* wake us up, savoring the moments of quiet before the teen noise drowned out her solace. Same for when I stayed at Tiffany's. But something weird was going on at this house.

"Wake up wake up wake up, Stacy!" her mom would sing like a homemade jingle. Then Stacy would groan.

"MOM! Leave us alone!"

Stacy's mom would continue by *grabbing Stacy's toes and singing the song more.*

For the life of me I can't figure out why this tradition was better than just letting us sleep in our growing teen bodies.

Spring break junior year rolled around, and Stacy and I spent the first weekend painting the set for our school's production of *Clue: The Musical*. The set looked cheap and bad. Four big wooden rectangles would come out interchangeably and assemble a different part of the iconic game board. The musical is also terrible, though, so it was fine. Volunteering for the crew of the show was an excuse for me to fawn over Mr. Raney. But that weekend was the only public engagement I had planned for my week off school.

Dipping her brush in yellow paint, Stacy yelled, "My family is going camping this week! You should come! We have a trailer that hooks up to my dad's truck so it's not even like we're really camping. You should come!"

That was the tip off. The refrain of "you should come!" I knew she wasn't going to let this idea go. I tried to change the subject, but it just kept changing back.

"Plus it'll be fun, we can hike and eat hot dogs and take

naps," she gushed. None of this sounded like what I wanted to do with someone else's family for the better part of a vacation. If I had my way I'd be waking up around noon to watch *Dawson's Creek* reruns on TBS.

I saw the RAV4 pull up and I got in the back seat. Instead of driving off, Mom rolled down the window to Stacy's smiling face.

"Can Akilah come camping with us this week?" Stacy asked, oblivious to the subtext that I *hated* this idea.

Looking back at me through the rearview mirror, I'm certain my mom noticed me mouthing "no" and shaking my head. So it can be considered no less than traitorous that she said, "Yeah, that should be fine, I'll bring her over," before we started the drive home.

"What the hell, Marilynn?" I began.

"Oh, come on, Kilah, it'll be fun!" she said, and then burst into laughter. She knew there was no way I was going to enjoy myself in the woods with little to no cell service for an undisclosed number of days with Stacy's family. She hadn't really met them, but she knew I was a frequent guest in their house and that if Stacy was any indication, they were super safe and square.

The trip was doomed from the jump. For starters: I didn't want to be there. Additionally, the entire drive to middle-of-nowhere Indiana was a drag. Stacy wouldn't

stop tattling on her little brother so we all lost movie priv-
ileges (yes, they were the kind of white people with the
TVs on the back of the car seats). I'd already seen *Chicago*,
but it's really not the kind of movie you can just stop in the
middle.

Once at the campgrounds, things only got worse and
more boring. We drove right out of cell range, and while
Stacy was a good friend for sitting and watching TV, without the help of background noise she could be too quiet.
Between eating our gas station bounty of sour gummies
and chips, we'd just nap for an hour or so at a time and then
wake the other up to not have to sit alone in the trailer with
our thoughts.

After enough rounds of this, Stacy thought it would be
best if we went on a hike.

"Fine," I said, when I really meant, "I'd rather get hit
by a car."

It was muddier than any of us expected, so we all had to
pretend we weren't pissed off that our shoes had been ren-
dered completely unwearable in public. There were more
hills and trees than we expected, so walking took forever.
Stacy's brother, Blaine, was struggling hard, and though I'm
no outdoorsperson, I certainly will not be pulling up the
rear in the event a bear, wild boar, or drunk dude catches
our scent.

"Is this pot?" Stacy asked, holding up a plant she'd found while we waited for Blaine to catch up.

"Yes," I lied, hoping that would end the conversation. And it did. *Kind of.* She ate it. She just shoved it in her mouth. And then, when she didn't like the taste, she thought she was going to throw up, which caused her great distress. She had a panic attack.

At that very moment, Blaine decided it would be a great idea to jump in a puddle that was deeper than he thought and proceeded to fall in, get soaked, and start to cry.

So now I'm in the woods with a damp ten-year-old and a panicking fourteen-year-old when all I wanted was to watch my shows at home in peace.

When we made it back to the campsite, there was more familial bickering to be endured. Stacy didn't want a hot dog, but all there was were hot dogs. She wanted s'mores, but it wasn't s'mores time yet. Blaine wouldn't stop crying. Their dad took him to the bathroom to presumably yell at him some more.

This whole time I just toasted bun after bun and made hot dog after hot dog. I didn't know if we were going to eat a whole pack as a unit, but I wanted the work part of the trip to be over already. Out of the darkness a tiny *meow* caught our attention.

A few moments later, a kitten with a broken back leg

wandered up to our campfire. It was cute, I'll concede. Was it pick-it-up-and-let-it-piss-on-your-hoodie cute, Stacy? I don't think so. So that was a whole thing.

Blaine and his dad came back from the bathroom, and they both looked like they'd seen a ghost.

"There were bloody handprints. Everywhere. On the walls. On the door," Stacy's dad recounted.

"Eww," I said.

"Oh my god, but I have to use the bathroom," Stacy said.

"Pee behind the trailer; none of us is going back to that bathroom!" her dad ordered, and now it was back to pouting and hot dogs while a literal murder may have been unfolding just steps away.

We ate s'mores mostly in silence because Stacy forgot the amp for her guitar (thank GOD). Around what was probably only nine p.m. we got bored of each other and decided we should go to sleep. Unfortunately I couldn't get comfortable. None of us could. There was rustling outside, and that murderer was probably on to us.

Plus, it was still kind of cold in the evening, but the bed that Stacy and I shared wasn't close enough to the heater for it to be effective. Stacy would insist on trying to be the big spoon, but then I'd get sweaty and have to push her off, desperate for this hell-trip to end.

And end it did. By three a.m. her father was having a

full-blown asthma attack because someone (I really don't know who) didn't clean out the heater filter, and dusty air had been blowing at full velocity into this man's lungs for hours. I let him take a hit off my inhaler, and we began the long drive back to the 'burbs.

I will always be best friends with Tiffany. She's so smart, so funny, so driven. As much as both of our leaves keep changing, she's the person I call when I get into town, and we pick up where we left off. I was in her wedding, and if I can con a man into settling down with me, she will be in mine. In relationships and friendships, it's important to really see the other person for who they are, their faults and all. And it's also important to know when those faults are too much.

In Stacy's case, years after we were both out of high school and college, she fell in love with a guy. I never met the guy, but he was good-looking in a way where he was definitely treated better his whole life. With women I tend to think, regardless of how attractive they are, that there was a period when they didn't know, or they didn't believe it. Men don't make it to their twenties without knowing they're good-looking. So there's that. As their relationship progressed, Stacy adopted some of his more backward, racist beliefs. We stopped being friends the day I read a post of hers on Facebook claiming that being big and black (in the case of slain teen Michael Brown) was, in its own way, "being armed." Yeah.

But it wasn't easy walking away. It hasn't been easy watching her get married and have kids with this guy. And the truth is she was always nice to me. Her family never treated me differently and always helped me whenever I needed it. When I think about friendship and love, I think that it really comes down to gray areas; love is the ability or willingness to see the other's gray areas—the spots where maybe you have to give them the benefit of the doubt, or let them grow into being something else. Love is lost when you can no longer do that. Though I'm aware Stacy really has always just wanted to be in love, and would say *anything* to be seen as the perfect match, there is no gray area when it comes to my lived experience. I just couldn't see a way forward for that friendship, and I don't regret it.

All this to say that Mindy Kaling is right, and some bitches just don't make the cut.

Bad Skin

You know you've had acne when you have very specific memories of zits:

That one time during the seventh-inning stretch at a major league baseball game, when you raised your arm and a twinge of pain notified you of the planet forming in an ingrown hair. The rest of the game you tried to covertly push your arm fat into your armpit, and by the bottom of the ninth there was a satisfying, almost audible "pop" letting you know that the tyranny was over. At least until tomorrow/the next month/forever. Acne is a life sentence, and it's one of the only "flaws" that we as a society refuse to embrace.

I remember my first zit. As a sedentary couch-child, I

took a lot of naps on the weekends. My mom usually spent the day running errands, and us kids liked to spend most of our time alone. For some reason I was especially tired that specific Sunday. Perhaps the whole prior day of watching television and eating chips had exhausted me. Either way, I made my way upstairs (with my comforter that I had taken downstairs to the couch, for extra comfort) to my bed and napped on and off for approximately eight hours. Waking up only to relieve myself, I noticed a pearl on the skin above my upper lip in the "snot trough," as my mom had so lovingly deemed that part of my anatomy. It's amazing that I knew exactly what had to be done, given my lack of experience, but I pressed both my pointer fingers into it, watching a tiny Silly String of zit goo escape. Convinced my skin inconveniences were behind me, I took my lazy ass back to bed.

. . . Until the next time I had to use the restroom. I woke up, walked back to the bathroom, and to my dismay, the pearl had returned. Was my earlier triumph a dream? I'd beaten the boss character, what more could he want with me?

I repeated the pressure technique, but this time I didn't let up. And the line of gunk just kept coming. My eyes began to water from the pain, but I knew that I couldn't be bothered by this after my next nap session. My tolerance for repeat performances is incredibly low. Eventually it would be Monday and I'd have to show up in fourth grade with the prepubescent baby skin of my classmates. Despite my completely open nap schedule, I didn't have time for this.

Finally a big glump came out, followed by the red blood of a champion. That *had* to be all. I waddled back to my twin-size bed, proud of having achieved so much that day. Perhaps that doesn't sound like a monumental day, just naps and zit-popping, but it's now in a chapter in a book, where it is immortalized forever.

Other notable zits include:

1. The one I popped in my purple locker mirror freshman year of high school, right before my crush approached me to ask about the world civ homework, none the wiser.

2. An ear zit that *definitely made a sound* after a week of driving me crazy.

3. A zit on my downstairs area that I only discovered after the most painful wipe of my life.

4. The pile of blackheads that pushed out of

my nose like that Play-Doh hair toy from the '90s during my first round of Accutane in college.

5.   The one in the middle of my back that I had to do a yoga position to finally eject.

6.   The beauty mark that was never a beauty mark but probably a decade-old blackhead.

7.   The secret eyebrow one that popped as I was filling in the hairs with my brow pencil. Ouch.

8.   Any number of boob zits.

9.   The one that showed up in the middle of my nose that decided to leave a chocolate chip scar there for about a year.

The truth is bad zits happen to good people. Mine are less for lack of hygiene (my pillow cases are among the cleanest you'll ever find) and more to do with raging hormones. Every single month without fail I will get a giant pustule on my chin and wonder how it could be happening to me (as if it hasn't happened every month before for the past sixteen years), and then boom, my period comes to town, ruining sheets and moods in its wake.

Birth control kind of helped, in the way that gaining weight and crying all the time helps.

Accutane definitely assisted in drying out everything (everything), excessive joint pain, general lethargy, and giving me a lifetime struggle with night blindness (that's right, for any teens reading this, the acne prescription you already have to log on to a website and take a quiz to get each month has a LOT of epic side effects your dermatologist may have forgotten to mention). If it's dark out, my eyes might as well be closed because nothing's gonna stop me from walking into a ditch or into the mouth of a bear or other things that lie in wait in the shadows. Mostly, though, I just bruise my shins on my late-night walks to the fridge. It hasn't deterred my ice cream habit, but it sure tries.

My favorite thing about having acne as an adult (no, acne doesn't magically go away on your eighteenth birthday, like you may have been led to believe) is the unsolicited advice. People love weighing in on other people's ailments. Have you ever tried to do anything? There's someone with a superiority complex just waiting to relate their unrelated experience to yours.

"I'm thinking of going to the gym more."

"You should try CrossFit! You're wasting your time if you do anything else, honestly. I feel like my full body workouts . . ." blah blah ad infinitum.

"I've been feeling anxious lately."

"Yoga!" they'll scream directly into your mouth. "And acupuncture! Needles will help with your anxiety! Do you drink tea? It's Instagram's fault! Stop eating gluten!" etc., etc.

"I have hormonal imbalances that cause my skin to sometimes get cystic acne."

"You should wash your face with . . ."

"No, I said it was my hormo—"

"Have you tried glycolic acid?"

Anyone with legit acne will tell you that yes, we've tried everything. I'm an expert. I don't have any questions. I know exactly what every damn acid does and doesn't do, which one requires you to wear sunscreen after, exactly how long a mask should be left on (sheet and clay), and I never, ever, ever need to hear from anyone about any new serum. All the serums already exist; they're just selling you more of the same garbage!

A guy once stayed over at my apartment and came out of the bathroom, mouth agape.

"Are all those products just for you? I just have soap!" he exclaimed in astonishment, as if he had walked into the sand tiger from *Aladdin*, never seeing such wonders before in his life.

Yes, I have at least five but no more than ten toners, face washes, face scrubs, special face scrubbers, peels, masks, creams, gels, tonics, and exfoliators. I wouldn't call myself a hobbyist, but I certainly spend more time than I'd like trying to figure out how to clear up my skin. In fact, almost all of my 11:11s and 12:34s have been spent wishing for clearer skin, longer eyelashes, and less cellulite. Sorry, world peace, someone else is gonna have to be less selfish with their wishes.

Body positivity has yet to reach out to those of us with pustules and pimples. Even with the number of social media accounts dedicated to high-def macro lenses filled with dermatologists squeezing and prodding the afflicted acne-sufferers for bigger, darker, grosser puss balls, the people suffering haven't been humanized. It's a new-age freak show with captions like "little zit, big squirt" and "removal of a twenty-five-year-old blackhead."

While having acne hasn't ever been told to me directly as a reason someone didn't want to date me or be my friend, it certainly ruined my self-esteem for years. Especially when the acne was on my back and chest as a teenager and I felt like I was inherently gross. The amount I loved myself truly increased every day my skin was slightly less bumpy than the day before. Even now, when I get a rogue forehead zit, I question if I should go out for fear of being photographed and having the shallow pits of hell on the internet feast on my misfortune.

But I'm also well-adjusted enough to know that everybody gets acne, at some point, and sometimes if you are blessed with baby-ass skin in high school, you're not immune to a battle with your skin later in life. The number of friends I envied at age fifteen for being walking magazine covers, Photoshopped by God for our eyes' consumption, ended up prematurely wrinkled, with rosacea, excess hair, and yes, sometimes a big fat zit in their twenties and thirties. There's no amount of water you can drink that is going to solve for your hormones changing and surging and depleting. There's no snake oil you can sell people who know the truth.

And honestly, I wish the only bad thing about me was my bad skin. That would be a pretty solid legacy, to be honest.

Disney

Handsome, unattainable man Ryan Gosling once said, "I'm in a relationship with Disneyland." When I first saw the GIF of this statement, I realized that I had this in common with him and we should be married forthwith. We're not and aren't going to be, but I, too, know the deep feeling of being enamored with the mouse.

I used to work at Disney World, which is not Disneyland. There aren't enough numbers to count how many times people respond with "The one in Florida?" when I tell them about my employment at the parks. Disney World is the *only* Disney World. There are Disneyland resorts in Paris, Shanghai, and Tokyo. All of these are modeled after Walt's original park in Anaheim, California. But that's not what we're discussing. We're discussing the WORLD of Disney—and how I ended up being a Disney person.

If one were to generalize, it would be easy to say that "Disney people" are a little much. They have kids or they are kids at heart. They share endless articles from clickbait websites about fan art imagining the princesses as everything from coat hangers to types of fish. They sing "Let it Go" at karaoke. I get it. Those people sound more basic than an Ugg boot. But that's not the kind of Disney person I am (and hopefully not the kind of Disney person handsome, unattainable Ryan Gosling is). Sometimes you *become* a Disney person. For some it happens the first time you go to Disney World. For some it happens working in the parks.

At the beginning of *The Lion King* on VHS, there's a commercial about two very cute little white boys who are packing to go to Disney World. The older brother (maybe seven) has already been and is feverishly telling the younger one what to expect. Hindsight is twenty-twenty, but I had no concept of being rich or poor back then, and obviously these kids had some serious generational wealth to have more than one Disney trip in their childhood. And you may be thinking, "Well, maybe they live in Florida and have a season pass," which is an interesting theory, but half of the commercial is kids packing suitcases. If you lived in Florida and had the pass, would you really be concerned about getting a hotel when you could just drive there for a day trip? I'm just saying.

After the older brother detailed how big Goofy is (which is roughly "can kick Dad's ass" big), Lanie and I decided that we were definitely asking for a trip to Disney World.

And so we did.

"Maybe," my mom said. This was years before I realized that *maybe* always means "I don't want to say 'no,' but absolutely not."

In high school my mom had to go to a conference in Florida and her group stayed at a Disney resort. She didn't get to go to the parks (tragic), but she did get the benefits of a Disney room card and she gushed about how when she called the front desk, after they solved her problems, they'd tell her, "Have a Magical Day!"

My days were painfully devoid of magic in Kentucky, but one day all of that would change, thanks in part to the only Disney princess to wield a sword, Mulan.

My senior year of high school was a little surreal. Junior year I auditioned for our Concert Choir. The group was notably the only choir that sang. Unfortunately they had the ugliest costumes and never danced. *The least dateable*. And since I was fourteen and aware of the fact that I was younger than everybody and one of the only black people any of the kids at my school had ever met, I knew there was no point in trying out for Girls' Ensemble (hot cheerleaders, but maybe they still had braces or highlights too chunky in their hair), or Show Choir (the only coed choir that featured the hottest guys from football lip-syncing with the hottest girls from cheerleading and the dance team).

I was Concert Choir attractive. I went into the audition and sang "Reflection," a Christina Aguilera ballad from the *Mulan* soundtrack.

I dozed off waiting for the cordless phone to ring with good news from the music teacher telling me I'd be adding choir to my ever-growing list of extracurriculars. All of my friends made it, but I didn't.

To this day I don't know why I didn't make it. I especially don't know why because my senior year in the spring (a semester into being a member of the Concert Choir), Ms. Bart announced we'd be doing a Disney-themed concert. In addition to announcing a solo opportunity for Concert Choir, she also told us we'd be dancing.

Like the cooler girls in the other choirs. Us. Dancing. *Imagine.*

A week or so later, she held auditions for the solo in that concert. Perhaps you've figured out where I'm going with this and that the song she chose was "Reflection," the Christina Aguilera ballad from the *Mulan* soundtrack.

The auditions were in the middle of class, with girls passing notes and lying around onstage while Ms. Bart lined up those who wanted to audition. I watched as girl after girl butchered the song. Soprano, alto, bad singer who made the cut—they all sounded as if they had never seen the movie. After about forty-five minutes of this nonsense, I decided I had nothing to lose by auditioning. I'd already experienced this exact, literal rejection. I was ready.

And I hit every note like I was Whitney goddamn Houston.

When I got done singing, the class clapped for me. I'm not joking. It was like at the end of a movie when people are celebrating because the protagonist reached their fullest potential. This was my freeze-frame fist-pump John Hughes Brat Pack moment.

Ms. Bart didn't waste time giving me the solo. We'd have two concerts and then tour the songs at the local middle and elementary schools.

I liked this new reputation of being a good singer. I liked the poetic justice of knowing I was always good at singing that damn song and that not making it into choir junior year must have just been a fluke. But much like

Mulan's newfound confidence after chopping her hair off and being a hot boy, things wouldn't work out exactly as I planned. The first concert went swimmingly (yay!), but the second performance was to be on a Wednesday, and I wasn't going to be able to make it (boo!) because it landed precisely on the day my mother proposed we fly to Florida to check out Bethune-Cookman College as a potential option, bringing me the closest I'd ever been to Disney.

I don't remember much about actually visiting Bethune-Cookman. I'm sure it's a great school, and I have a number of the HBCU's marching band's showcases on my YouTube workout playlist. What I *do* remember about the trip was flying on a plane for the first time and learning that you shouldn't wear shorts and flip-flops on a plane, regardless of how warm it is where you're going. I also remember spending the evening at Downtown Disney.

Downtown Disney isn't in a park; it's kind of like a lavish strip mall. A Ghirardelli, an Earl of Sandwich. The Florence Mall in Kentucky could never. The largest and most appreciated store of all is World of Disney. It stretches forever, and in a few years I would know that Disney is mostly gift shops anyway, so this *was* an authentic experience.

Mom bought a disposable camera and snapped away.

"Oh my god, they have the *villains*?!?!" I screeched,

gesturing to the row of snow globes that featured Ursula and Scar.

"What movie is that from?" my mom asked, oblivious to the fact that I'd committed these entire films to memory and thought of them before any actual true-life circumstances when asked to recount my childhood. The first film I saw in theaters was *A Goofy Movie*. *Snow White* got stuck in our VCR (my mom still has this VCR in the garage). I remember that we ate Whopper Jr.'s from Burger King for dinner the first night we watched *The Lion King*. The next school year started with me in a fresh new pair of Pocahontas shoes from Payless. Walt Disney is probably rolling in his grave thinking how happy he made a little black girl at the end of the twentieth century.

Back in the store, I tried on so many hats. There's a great picture of me with a "Rasta Mickey" hat on. It was a little racist. I know. But I was just so happy to be experiencing life among the wealthy dreamers in sunny Orlando instead of singing for an audience of my friends' parents again that I let it slide.

The biggest city I'd ever been to was Cincinnati, so seeing something so far from my hometown really impacted me. I had my first taste, and I knew I'd be back.

* * *

The spring of my sophomore year of college was a drag. I hated all of my friends, my roommate was getting on my last nerve, my classes were all required but in no way guiding me toward a career I wanted. I needed a vacation. Honestly, I hadn't been on a vacation in three years, and before that it had been my whole life. I was rundown, irritable. I needed relief, but I also needed to graduate on time so I could spend more of my time doing what I wanted to do. This led me to searching for summer internships and asking anyone I could for advice.

No dice. But I started to comb my memory for any glimmers of hope offered to me by upperclassmen of years gone by. There was one guy, Jonathan, who told me at a party (where we were a bit tipsy off of really gross coconut rum) about his ex-girlfriend that he met at Disney World.

He opened his laptop and went to a folder marked "Disney" and started clicking around.

"You won't believe how pretty she is," he told me. I found it strange that he was being so complimentary of an ex to a near-stranger at a party.

He flipped the computer around and awaited my reaction.

"She's a mermaid?!" I shouted, the coconut rum lowering my self-awareness.

"Well, she was during our internship."

The photo showed a girl with a bright red wig that didn't look *real* necessarily, but certainly wasn't cheap, with a purple clamshell bra and a green sequined tail sitting on a rock formation, huge blue eyes beaming. Next to her was a dorky guy that was blushing and appeared shorter because of the length of her tail. It was Jonathan.

"So, you dated a Disney princess?" I questioned.

"Yeah, we met on our internship," he said.

By this point I realized that my roommate wanted to leave, so I called her over to look at the picture before we peaced out.

"I've never seen *The Little Mermaid*." She shrugged, and we gathered our things and went back to the dorms.

Years later, as I was hoping for any sweet relief from small-town campus life, this memory struck me, and I started googling Disney internships. I found the Disney College Program—a six-month internship at either Disneyland or Disney World that offered housing, full-time employment, and communications and leadership courses for college credit.

My eighteen-year-old fingers had never filled out an application so fast. And within a few weeks I opened the golden ticket in the form of a big purple folder at the C-PO (college post office) that sealed my fate: I was going to Disney World—for six months starting in June!

"YES! I'M GETTING THE HELL OUT OF HERE I'M GOING TO DISNEY WORLD!" I screamed. No one yelled anything back. The lady at the café upstairs kept dropping fries and chicken tenders, the janitor swept the floor near the elevator. All at once everything was the same, but entirely different.

Once summer hit I joined the Facebook group for all of us lucky students around the world who had gotten their folders. We all posed for selfies with our folders and posted them in the group. Soon I was going to be down at Disney, away from my Podunk college town, and maybe dating a prince of my own.

I was the second roommate to arrive at our apartment in Vista Way. The college program had three apartment complexes, and Vista Way was the cheapest by several hundred dollars a week. In no position to waste money on having slightly fewer roommates, I moved in with five other girls. Four were American and one was the sweetest French girl who spoke hardly any English and would often clean up after everybody. We didn't deserve her.

Vista Way had a real reputation for being the party complex. People even say Vista Way in a sort of salacious tone, emphasizing the "way" part of the name. Two pools, each with its own hot tub, made this the place no one wanted to live, but everyone wanted to hang.

Sleep did not find me the night before training, but I quickly wished it had. Before they let you tour the park and ride some rides, you have to sit through the longest training sessions of all time with about forty other people who also just want to ride Space Mountain. By hour ten I had all but sworn allegiance to the mouse who was now my food, shelter, and family.

The best part of Traditions (the official name for the training) was learning all of the official slang and lingo of the park. Employees were *cast members*. Any time you were visible in spaces with guests, you were *onstage*, and any time you were in a storage closet or in the tunnels (*utilidor*) under the Magic Kingdom you were *backstage*. Pointing is rude unless you use both your middle and pointer fingers. We don't have good days, we have *magical* days. Rides are *attractions*. And we don't call a celebrity by their name unless we see it on their credit card at the end of their transaction. No cell phones. Ever.

Traditions was like being jumped into a gang, if that gang was populated by all the kids from high school forensics and glee club. I was told about how to wear my uniform (*costume*) and exactly how to get on the premises from the bus since there are no cars in the Magic Kingdom proper, only in the employee parking lot.

When I finally got to the morning of training where we got to go to the park, I had nearly forgotten that I was going to eventually be working at Walt Disney World Resort. I'd all but resigned myself to living out the rest of my days in that poorly lit conference room with the sexual harassment HR video.

My group of about ten students got to the Magic Kingdom gates an hour before the park opened. Only the front gate cast members would be allowed to use this entrance; the rest of us would take the tunnel to our respective *lands*. There were seven lands that we'd have to discover on our own time. We wandered down Main Street, U.S.A., and our trainer killed the magic of about nine hundred things at once. Pointing out what spaces were for storage, and why the castle looks so big when approaching it versus when you're leaving the park. I apparently didn't articulate that it was my first time at Disney very well in my interview, because this was brutal. It's like if you found roommates on Craigslist and you went to the apartment and it looked great, but then they told you the shower water was never warm, the outlets don't work, and that there's exactly one rat living there, but the rat is allotted two five-minute smoke breaks a day.

After a soul-crushing, brass-tacks morning, we were

sent to our respective lands for additional training sessions, and we finally got to ride an attraction. Though I worked in Tomorrowland, the line at Space Mountain was already too long, so we'd be riding Buzz Lightyear's Space Ranger Spin: a truly delightful ride/game that made me want to go home and watch *Toy Story* all over again.

After working in uneventful *"merchantainment"* for a few months, Disney announced that they were doing auditions for *entertainment* positions. Entertainment cast members at Disney are the peak of the hierarchy. They're the selected "pretty" few. If they wanted to cut you in line in the mouseketeeria, they totally could. They got to ride go-carts to their respective lands while I was stuck hoofing it in what was essentially a glorified dumpster under the Magic Kingdom.

This was exciting for a number of reasons, not the least of which was that Disney was just beginning to get more diverse. They were releasing a Tinkerbell movie that starred a black fairy! And an Asian fairy! And a coded-Latina fairy! When I'd started working at WDW, *The Princess and the Frog* hadn't even come out yet. There were no opportunities for me to be a "face character." And suddenly I had the opportunity to audition.

The auditions at Disney are always the same. You go into a wooden room save for floor-to-ceiling mirrors. A dance studio, basically. You're given a number, and when they call your group of twenty-five people, you line up in a couple of rows and smile. Then, a person with a demeanor similar to that of Meryl Streep's character in *The Devil Wears Prada* walks up to you and stares at your face. This may cause you to laugh or, in my case, wink? I wanted it bad, what can I say?

After a couple of minutes you leave and wait for them to call your number. This can be utterly devastating, as I'd learn a couple years later when I returned to Orlando after college and reauditioned. But that day *they called my number*! I couldn't believe it! I had really wanted them to, but the criteria (look like a fairy from a movie that hasn't been released yet) seemed too arbitrary for me to pass. But I did and I fit within the Disney height requirement (five-foot-four or less finally coming in handy) and everything!

The rest of that morning was a blur. If I remember one thing clearly it was that everyone who had gotten a callback was white except for me, and they all seemed like more experienced actors. As I sat in a makeup chair and had a woman apply gold and orange eye shadow and lashes to my face, another man dropped a script in my hand.

"You have to do a country accent. Can you do a country accent?" he asked.

"I'm from Kentucky, is that country enough?"

"Great! See you in ten." And with that he was gone.

"You should probably start reading it out loud?" the makeup lady suggested with the tonality of someone who could tell I was a total amateur.

All the other girls chosen were pacing and *loudly* reading their scripts. Immediately confident. Not afraid of messing up a line since it was a cold read. I was shrinking into myself, scared that I'd go in and freeze, or stumble. Content in my makeup chair spiral, a costuming employee handed me a dress.

I wriggled in, unsure how they knew my exact size but too timid to ask. As I exited the dressing room a woman was waiting for me.

"Put your hands against the wall," she said as if she were arresting me. Now truly scared, I obliged. It was then that she attached the twenty-pound wings to my back. So I wasn't just nervously pacing and trying to read the script above a whisper without attracting too much attention, but I was also trying to have a natural posture with four-foot-tall wings attached to my back.

I entered the dance studio again, three people sitting at a folding table with lots of paper on it. No warm welcome, just a nod to begin.

"Oh, Tank!" I started, my country accent over the top.

"Excuse me! Sorry, this character *doesn't* have an accent. She's just anxious," they corrected. *Same*, I thought. "Try again."

And I did, but it clearly wasn't good enough. I left my phone on vibrate as I changed and got ready to go back to my post in Tomorrowland. I bragged openly about the audition in the mouseketeeria. As I did, a very cute girl in those very same fairy wings walked in. And she looked good. And they'd clearly kept her there since the morning.

Shit.

I was bummed out, but this was also not my first time failing spectacularly. And it was still the closest any of my friends had come to becoming an entertainment cast member. I now knew it was possible. That it would really just come down to if I was confident in the room in the future. It's completely reasonable that this adulthood brush with auditioning and rejection helped build that frosty exterior that can shake off rejection at the highest level and stay motivated to keep trying.

After the audition didn't pan out, I ended up working the Space Mountain arcade. It was a particularly slow time in the parks due to the recession, and so I mostly just used the arcade keys to bust open the machines and give myself a few free games to eat up some of the time left on my shift. I was in the middle of a pretty intense round of Tekken 5 when I was tapped on my shoulder by a woman I recognized immediately.

"Hi, sorry, I was wondering where we go to check out? No one is at the counter . . ." she said, implying that she was trying to buy something.

As I rang up her tub of cotton candy, she noticed my name tag and asked, "Your name is Akilah? From Kentucky . . . Are you Marilynn's daughter???"

"Yeah! Hey!" I said.

It was my kindergarten teacher, Mrs. Sheldon. It had been thirteen years, but I guess we both looked eerily the same. Behind her stood two adorable little girls, the same in every way.

"It's my girls' birthday! They're eight today! It's August 8th, 2008, so we thought this would be the perfect time to make our way down here," she explained. I dipped into the secret supply of "magical moment" goodies and gave them both the extremely limited-edition Tinker-bell pin that could only be acquired by befriending a cast member.

It made their whole day.

Twenty minutes later when I was back in the tunnels under the Magic Kingdom at my locker, I called my mom to tell her how wild it was running into her.

"Yeah, it's probably like New York in that way. They say that if you wait on a corner in New York, everyone in the world will eventually pass you," my mom said. I don't know if people say that about New York for real, but at the time it made me feel like I was somewhere super important, and that the universe was trying to tell me that this was more than coincidence—that I needed to be somewhere people wanted to be.

The South

WHAT'S BEAUTIFUL ABOUT IT?

Biscuits.

WHAT'S BAD ABOUT IT?

Racism.

College Years

College wasn't for me. I did it. I got a degree, and I'm better for it—but I wasn't built for it.

From the street view the campus looks like any other. Old and new brick buildings sit on a large plot of green. The sidewalks splinter into higher and lower paths leading from educational facilities to living quarters. The town is small, quaint, with seemingly no downtown or uptown. Its sheer inoffensiveness is remarkably unremarkable. This would be my home for five years.

Berea College in Berea, Kentucky, was not top on my list of colleges to go to. In fact, though I'd spent my entire life in Kentucky, I didn't hear of the city or the college until my AP English teacher told me about it senior year of high school. She wasn't even specifically addressing me.

"It's my thirty-year college reunion this weekend," she said. I was busy counting on my fingers to try to figure out how old that must make her, but other students seemed genuinely interested in her life.

"What school did you go to?" Bob asked. I remember it was Bob because it seemed like a weird name for a seventeen-year-old. Still is.

She launched into an eager rant about how great Berea College was. How the tuition was free for low-income students who all work on campus. How the education was top-notch and the school had many famous benefactors. She urged us all to apply there, too.

Only one other girl and I took the time to do that. We both got in. I got into all of the schools I applied to, but only one of them had a price tag of "free," so that basically sealed the deal. After all, I was only making like $150 a week at Fazoli's. That's not even enough for one textbook's table of contents.

During those first days I got to know my new roommate, Morgan. Morgan was a hipster before being a hipster was a thing (she owned several beanies, ironic tees, and a succulent), and I immediately just assumed she was home-schooled (she was). During the summer she had sent me a cat-shaped card saying she couldn't wait to be my roommate, and we chatted briefly on AIM.

Morgan brought a lot of books with her to college, which I thought was bizarre. High school had pretty much murdered my love of recreational reading with all the required reading we had to do. I didn't know why she thought she'd have time to enjoy the written word outside all the classes, but she seemed adamant. She also had a ton of DVDs of shows that I had only heard of but never actually watched. *Veronica Mars* and others. CDs by Ani DiFranco, which were outside the realm of my pop culture upbringing. But considering it was a dry campus, I conceded that being outside my comfort zone would mean listening to *indie* music and seeing *indie* movies. It was also Kentucky, so going to a small, non-state school was already a weird choice. But I was committed to this new lifestyle.

After meeting a few more girls on my floor, we had a solid group of us to go to lunch or the mailbox with and explore the town together. Even though all of these changes seemed quick, what was most off about being a fish out of water was that I didn't even really recognize myself. In high school I joined whatever clubs I could. I wanted to be *part* of it. If there was a sign-up sheet within a ten-mile radius, I was committed to signing.

College was the first time I felt myself recoiling from the spotlight. I auditioned for the fall play, but after the first rehearsal I dropped out. I "ran" for house council in my dorm and became the first-floor representative, but I resented the meetings being two hours long and all about everyone's problems with the showers, the laundry room, and the curfew hours. It wasn't my class workload. I wasn't too busy exactly, but I did feel like I was wasting time. I was just not interested in giving myself to another thing without seeing how it might benefit me in return.

I even thought I'd lucked out with my on-campus job in public relations at the visitor's center. Anyone who ended up in Berea, Kentucky, could watch an informative video and receive pamphlets and maps of the town from us. My job was literally to search all newspapers for any mention of the school, cut the blurb out with scissors, and glue (with a glue stick) the article to a piece of paper and file it. That was it. I was the human equivalent of "command F." Oh, and I made $2.30 an hour.

The wages were that low because they were paying us out of the school's endowment and the rest of that money was funding our education. It's a smart system because it keeps the campus running on a budget and always bringing in profit.

Nothing felt like how I expected college to be. I thought I'd have more freedom, but having no money (so having very little to experiment with style, or buying music, or going out) and living in a town tinier than where I grew up made me feel like I was trapped in the smallness of it all. College was supposed to be acquiring a taste for cappuccino in smart blazers with elbow patches in Greenwich Village during the week and attending tailgating events on weekends. *My school didn't even have a football team.* Instead of getting a free weekend for Labor Day, we'd have to wait a couple more months for the school's "Mountain Day" celebration. It's what it sounds like: we all go climb a mountain and eat granola and generally do the things that now seem like cool day trips on Instagram but back then were just what boring people did.

In high school I felt like I could never have a "real" experience like in the movies, running around in school on a Saturday, trying to hide from the principal, or being the reluctant prom queen dating an unexpectedly nice hot guy— because I was black and two years younger and too much of a background character to ever have main character triumphs. In college I felt like all of that was possible for me, just at any other school. In hindsight, I know that I wasn't completely right about that—all of my friends who went to big state schools attest that it was a little bit different than what I imagined—but I felt like what I needed was a larger pool to swim in. Would you rather be a big fish in a small pond or a small fish with the potential to get bigger in a big pond?

I settled into my chill college routine in the four p.m. hour before dinner. Every day I'd find a free lounge in my dorm and turn the channel to ABC. There I'd be greeted by Oprah Winfrey. My obsession with the mogul began long before college (I mean, I was alive in the '90s and I'm not an idiot), but here was where I realized that *this*, broadcasting to an audience of millions, was a goal worth chasing.

Now, that seems vain as I reread it, but Oprah never ever seemed to be doing this *for* herself. Even on those episodes that were specifically about her struggles with her weight, the real meat of the show was that she was making it okay *for women* to have conversations out loud instead of thinking we were alone. It didn't even matter the subject. Oprah cared so genuinely and deeply that even guests with whom I shared no common ground made me really examine my life. There was an episode with a blind teenager who used echolocation to get around. After he miraculously made it across the stage (a stage with multiple drop-offs into the audience), he demonstrated this clicking sound he'd developed that he'd make with his tongue and simply wait for the echo to bounce back to him from other objects. Based on how long it took for the sound to come back to his ears he'd know if he was close to or far away from objects.

I suck at math. I can do basic shit, but I will do it slowly and use my fingers—and I just explained a mathematical method of survival for an ailment I've never had. *That's* the power of Oprah.

As the hour of television wrapped every day, I thought about how I could somehow become her. I'd taken her major (communications) and minor (theater) to heart when signing up for courses, and I'd read unofficial books about her front to back. I read all the books in her book club. I just had no idea how to turn all of that into a career as the next Oprah.

Simultaneous to my newfound love of all things Winfrey was the Lonely Island's grand debut on *Saturday Night Live* with their digital shorts. I'd spend almost all my evenings on Facebook and Myspace refreshing pages in hopes of discovering something worth talking about or reacting to. The weekend that "Lazy Sunday" dropped changed all of that.

I woke up late that Sunday and missed breakfast. When my roommate returned she couldn't shut up.

"Have you heard that Chronicles of Narnia song?!" she asked.

"A song about *The Lion, the Witch and the—*"

"No!" she cut me off, and then pulled up a clip on You-Tube.

It was at that moment that I realized that (1) I needed to just go ahead and sign up for a YouTube account; I was spending an increasing amount of time searching through the collection of unregulated '90s theme songs and weird animations, and (2) this is how I would become Oprah, or at least Oprah-adjacent enough that I could meet her one day; I would make comedy videos for the internet that were funny, thought-provoking, and, above all else, catchy. People would share them and I'd be the coolest kid on campus.

By the following semester I was already casting sketches for YouTube. Did I have a "content strategy"? No! I just uploaded videos to the account belonging to whoever had the fastest Wi-Fi. The videos would sometimes take hours to upload. They took even longer to write and shoot. And though none of the college videos went viral in today's sense, we made some campus-specific hits.

One such video is called "Pass the Plate - Chicken a la Spinach." You can probably still find it somewhere on a defunct YouTube channel. The premise was just a parody of a Disney Channel interstitial whereby a soccer ball is kicked from scene to scene, around the world, detailing how different cultures use ingredients. After noticing a distinct lack of diversity in these segments, we decided to make one about people in Atlanta and how they use spinach. Please don't make me describe the video further: do yourself a favor and go watch it.

The modicum of fame felt good. To be honest, at a school so small everyone was known for something, it felt good to be seen as a true original. No one else on my campus was making YouTube videos on purpose. It's scary calling yourself a filmmaker or a writer, or anything that demands proof of skill. I was just a kid with a camera, but my classmates saw me as a *storyteller*. My roommate was a photographer, so I already had the best five pictures uploaded to Facebook. Now that I'd pivoted to video, I was unstoppable.

Being back home for the summer, no one understood what the hell I was doing. As I set up a tripod and a camera in my room, my mom asked, "Are you making a porn?"

And I had to explain that no, I was not. I was making videos where I talked about stuff that annoyed me, or playing ukulele, or doing a simple hair tutorial. No one was making money from videos back then, so having hobbies that I then filmed and edited and uploaded seemed like a lot of work to anyone who wasn't in that world.

But that was the *best* of that world. That feeling of just

wanting to make something that was poignant, or different, or more artistic rather than what would get the most views (though views always sort of mattered) was the purest the internet could be. Being a person "on the internet" was still kind of *dorky*. People would ask why I spent so much time on my computer. They had no idea that the internet world was still the world, but it had inside jokes and etiquette and style. There was a divide between those of us who had been there since Neopets, making a home for our voices and our images and our design, and those who used their computers for emails and word processing. To go viral meant more back then. It hardly means anything now.

That's what college was for me. I learned a lot of things I've since forgotten (including how to use Excel for math purposes, how to apply for financial aid, and how to write ten pages in a single night). I keep in touch with a few friends from college, but what I really got out of it was a passion. I learned to like *making* stuff, even after a long day. I learned to be funnier, punchier, and better at all the internet stuff. I learned to edit videos and photos and audio and crashed so many cheap crappy computers into dust. I figured out what the rest of my life (or at least my twenties) would be about, irrespective of my choice of major. So yeah, while college wasn't *for* me, getting through it and finding my true passion was worth it.

Getting Too Good at
Your Plan B

In every creative person's life, there is a crossroads. It's a moment when they realize that they've been doing their day job, well, for a sufficient span of time (be that months or years) and that they now have to decide:

Will they continue pursuing what they love after hours *or* will they settle into their backup career and abandon their dreams on a neglected shelf of their own potential?

This decision is usually thrust upon the dreamer by way of a promotion, or a relationship, or anything that would demand the attention of those imaginative brain cells to the detriment of pursuing that "road less traveled." It's a formative, vulnerable moment whereby an otherwise rational person thinks, *Huh, but I'm pretty good at my job, and health insurance is a good enough reason to hate my life.* And in that moment, you can cut and run from what always felt like a mediocre placeholder for what you actually want to do, or you can lean into the mundane and opt to have a small but comfortable life. For me, this ultimatum came at noon on a Monday surrounded by pie.

Two years before the pie incident, I had just moved back home to Kentucky from Florida. The media would inaccurately describe this phenomenon as "boomeranging." The idea was that after graduating college, us wittle, coddled babies missed the teat and after being shoved into the "real world" returned home to purposely avoid having to grow up. The truth wasn't so convoluted: millennials were graduating into the eye of the recession, and paper degrees from renowned universities proved to be not so buoyant.

It was 2010, and after a miserable eight months of post-graduation poverty in Orlando—never squelched no matter how many jobs (three) or Craigslist gigs (countless) I suffered—I threw my hands in the air and returned to the Bluegrass State if only to make enough money (sans rent bill) to stop the incessant collection calls regarding my never-used, still in-the-box degree.

The opportunity to jump the Disney ship came after I sent my résumé to the Museum Center in Cincinnati on a whim one evening. The pay was $50,000 (a fortune to me, a girl sleeping on an inflatable mattress) and would offer me freedom to create videos, take photos, and run the social media sites for the massive institution. I had an initial phone interview (taken on my Net10 phone because my Blackberry got stolen at work one night) and immediately was asked to come in for an IRL interview.

"I'm moving home in a few weeks, so this is perfect. I can fly home early to meet with you," I lied. But I needed a job. I needed them to believe me so I could pull myself up by my bootstraps, even though at this point I didn't even have boots.

Anything I could sell, I did: a table in my room, a side table from Ikea, a few lamps and picture frames. I left a duvet, and any clothes that were too thick to fit in my suitcases, and a note on the fridge that I was moving on. My roommates understood, as our lease was up in a month and only half of the apartment was still on a speaking basis because Clarice brought bed bugs into our home and refused to pay for it.

I bought my ticket at the airport, cashing in on a three-hundred-dollar insurance settlement after being rear-ended the year before. In hindsight, that whiplash and ambulance ride were a true blessing in disguise. Sometimes my neck still gets sore, but I needed that three hundred dollars to get the eff out of Florida.

After I unpacked, my mother drove me to the job interview (I had sold my car to afford moving to Florida and had no way of buying a new one). I wore what I called my "interview outfit": a red jacket with three-quarter-length sleeves and chic black buttons, and a black-and-white-checkered dress with black flats. I smiled and seemed interested and gave them ideas for how to build a presence online that matched their presence in the community.

I didn't get the job. My social media predilection did not prove equal to actual experience in social media marketing.

There was so much embarrassment in coming back. I've grown enough to realize that no one was so consumed with my whereabouts or whyabouts, but at the time it felt like all of my internet acquaintances could smell my sadness. Every question about why I moved back home felt less curious than accusatory. *Everyone thinks you're a failure. They know you didn't "make it" in Orlando* was the song stuck in my head every time I browsed back to Facebook.

This feeling of utter loserdom compounded when the only job I could find immediately upon returning home was at the Justice in the mall. Justice as a store is fine. It's an explosion of pink and purple and sparkles designed to empty the bank accounts of every parent of a cool girl aged zero to thirteen. If there's a doll, lip gloss, candy, band, or hair accessory worth coveting in those middle school halls, it was purchased at Justice.

When I was a kid, Justice was called Limited Too, and I was always too fat and poor for their clothes. There was no point in buying a twenty-dollar T-shirt that I would outgrow over the course of a lazy summer, and because I hit puberty a full two years before most of my peers, the clothes always took on a pornographic appearance on my body. I hated that store. But to add insult to injury: I was twenty-one, and I was working in the same mall I did when I was fifteen.

I was grateful for the paycheck and got to work with my friends from my summer stint at Forever 21 four years prior, but I needed *real* money. If I was to be covered head to toe in glitter of my own volition, I needed to be making more than eight dollars an hour. My mom had to drive me to and from work every day, and she charged me gas money. This was understandable, but it took my weekly earnings down to three hundred dollars, and there was no viable way out.

Every night after work I'd come home and get on my three-year-old dinosaur Dell laptop and pray that it hadn't accrued another virus. I'd spend hours each night copying and pasting my cover letter into message fields and meticulously combing through to make sure the addressee was consistent with the application. Sometimes these sessions would last hours and would only end after I too quickly applied for a job, sending the uninspiring "please see my résumé attached" note without attaching a résumé.

I wasn't making YouTube videos, either. While I had uploaded a few back in Orlando, my fifty-dollar webcam had given up, and after breaking my camera and selling it for dinner one night, I had no way of shooting and editing anything.

Lost, desperate, and tired of having a degree burning in my pocket, but apparently not being qualified yet to work the cash register, I made my full-time job applying for jobs. One evening after work I checked my inbox and had a message from a local water and coffee company. They'd liked my résumé and cover letter and wanted me to come in for an interview.

The next day I called out of work, suited up (the red jacket/checkered dress combo), and rode shotgun to a suburb north of Cincinnati to the quaint warehouse with offices adjacent.

A bell sounded as I opened the door to the building, and a homely woman with a few missing teeth asked me if I was picking up or dropping off. Confused, I told her that I was there for an interview.

"Oh! I'll get Bobby!" she said, buzzing me into the office.

The room seemed like a small set for an '80s movie. Everyone there had that sort of poofy front bang you only see in less cosmopolitan places and fit perfectly in their beige cubicles and dark carpet—the kind of carpet I only remember seeing in preschool and doctor's office waiting rooms. I'd hate to put Orlando on a pedestal, but even that city had made the switch back to hardwood floors by now and this was all too retro.

Bobby came to meet me only a moment later and escorted me into the conference room that, too, felt confusingly old. He was a tall, handsome man in his early forties with reddish hair and an enormous smile. I took my seat, and Roger, a slightly older man with salt-and-pepper hair and glasses, joined.

I assumed since I had the CEO and the CFO present we'd begin the interview, but we waited for a woman named Helga. She lumbered into the room and sat down in a huff, giving off a terrible, sea-witch first impression.

"All right! All right, let's get started," she sneered. I immediately disliked her.

You know that thing where you meet a person and there's just something about them, their face, their smell, the way they look at you, *something*, that just gives you an intuitive desire to avoid them at all costs even though you're trying not to judge a book by its cover? It was like that.

And you should trust that instinct. The line of questioning was standard but long-winded, and my mind drifted, picturing Marilynn driving back toward Kentucky, tired of waiting an hour for her kid to dazzle a bunch of strangers at a company she's never heard of.

But finally, Bobby popped the question.

"Is thirty-five thousand enough?" he offered. I tried to be cool about it.

"Yeah, that sounds about right."

And with that I was shaking hands and grabbing a free cup of coffee, and Bobby even walked out to the car to meet my mom, who hadn't left my ass in a moment of weakness or for something to help her diabetic blood sugar from going too low.

It wasn't *all* downhill from there. I got my own big sunlight-drenched office that I could decorate however I wanted. Bobby knew that I couldn't be a star social media manager without a Mac computer, an iPad, a brand-new DSLR camera, and a company Blackberry. In an instant I had everything I needed to make my dreams come true.

Well, my mom was still driving me to work every day, which became a teaseable offense in the office. I was the youngest employee by at least a decade, the only black person not working in the warehouse, and no one understood me. Helga seethed with jealousy, immediately becoming the meanest of the bunch. Why didn't *she* have a private office? How come *her* computer was an old PC like everyone else's?

The sad part is I get it. I'd be pissed, too, if I worked somewhere for fifteen years and after five minutes some new, non-sea-witch girl got all the fun toys and privacy. I *get it*. But I also get that it's not my fault she didn't have her own office and that she had no idea how to work Apple products. I am a feminist, I think women should have everything men get, but I also wasn't about to give up being doted on to a woman with no manners, who burped out loud in the office and who started all of the drama, all while being alarmingly unaware of how long her nose hairs had gotten.

One major plus of my mom being a saint and driving me forty miles to work every day was that we got closer.

"I didn't make thirty-five thousand till I was in my thirties." She beamed. We'd spend our car rides thinking about how to decorate the office, what cool accessories young tech people would have, and how to really *be* the role. I've found that the solution to imposter syndrome for me is to treat life like a scene in a movie. Oh, I'm not ready to build a local brand into *the* local brand on Facebook? Well, I look damn good in these new, trendy clothes and will spend any downtime at work reading articles by more educated people about the work I'm supposed to be doing.

And I did do work. Sure, it was mostly writing my own blog and editing videos and pictures I'd use on my own social accounts to try to become an influencer, but I also created all the social media accounts and ran successful contests and giveaways and made the newsletters and promotional content beautiful. Plus, keeping up the appearance of working hard when Helga and others burst in the door without knocking was its own full-time job.

After a month or two I'd saved enough money to buy a laptop for editing my pictures and videos. I'd had the company get the programs I'd need to stay competitive online. Adobe Creative Suite, Microsoft Office. Just a couple months after that I'd buy a Nissan Cube with high payments, thanks to my dumpy credit from not having gainful employment straight out of school.

It's crazy to me that in America we're expected to pay back our education immediately. Six months is not a buffer. Six months isn't long enough to get a promotion at most jobs, so why on earth would we implore people to pay back thousands of dollars before they have it? What a nightmare.

Anyway, it took me nine months to really be sick of the job. I'd gotten back on my feet, I went from owing everybody money to owing everybody less money, and people were starting to ask me to write for their blogs. I'd come to an impasse: I could continue down this path, find myself at this company twenty years later, having slowly turned into a sea witch, but having made enough money to feel successful in my hometown. I could marry a guy I went to high school with, send my kids to the same schools I'd gone to. Never vacation farther than Chicago. Be in bed early on weeknights and go out to the same bars every weekend. I'd built a great group of friends around myself. My friend Erica would always be the coolest person in Cincinnati and would help me meet bands that toured through our town and I'd get free drinks forever. It wasn't totally unappealing. That would have been enough.

But just like in college, I had expectations for my life, and I was done feeling stifled by my means and my location. I wanted an opportunity to really compete. I wanted a YouTube video with more than a few thousand views. I wanted to start fresh somewhere no one knew me and then make them meet me. And to me, that was New York. It was Brooklyn. It was living with strangers, and learning the subway system, and being young and broke among artists, not young and well paid for the area and staying in my mom's house until I found love or she got tired of me. I wanted mythical young adulthood. I wanted to take a risk and feel success on my terms.

So I saved for a few more months, I gave notice, and with two suitcases and a couple grand in my pocket, I took the leap. I could see how the rest of my life would play out in Cincinnati. I decided not knowing in New York would be a better option.

How to Literally Get
to New York

Why does bus travel sound so romantic? Like trains in a Wes Anderson movie, buses always seem like a beautiful, vintage way to see America. Flying above for a few hours, America just looks like a poorly sewn together pattern of greens and browns with the occasionally stunning blue lake or less stunning brown river. It's too far away to look like anything meaningful.

No, it's buses that give you a gritty view of what America is really like. Passing schools, churches, and mom-and-pop restaurants and taking highways with numbers that don't quite fit together like the familiar ones in your state. When you're riding along, you can take in the signs welcoming you to states personally, with some colorful cursive on a bridge or in the middle of the woods.

This is what I convinced myself when I tried to find a ticket from Cincinnati to New York. "Who can beat a thirteen-hour trip with so much *charm* and for only ninety dollars?" Surely, if I had an extra four hundred dollars to spare, flying in a middle seat next to the bathroom would have been far more charming.

I knew I was going to move to New York, but after moving to Orlando with no employment lined up and the desperation of asking the insurance company of the woman who rear-ended me months prior for a paltry three hundred dollars for the whiplash/to pay my rent on time for once, I knew I had to have a job or at least a sense of how to get one before I could leave home again.

For weeks I scoured New York's Craigslist job ads, trying to decide if I could justify leaving a cushy job in Cincinnati and living rent free (but paying the cable bill and for my car each month, to be sure) to start over in America's largest city, filled with talented people who probably went to that *Fame* high school, able to meet people with apartments not in basements while figuring out how to get headshots and also discern good coffee from boiled floor remnants.

I wasn't super convinced of my abilities to do or be any of those things, but I wanted to be as sure as I could be before I made the move. Scrolling became my favorite after (and during) work activity. How much would an apartment cost with three roommates? How much would I have to make to be able to afford everything and also be able to actually buy things for myself every once in a while? I did the algebra that in high school they told us we'd use every day for the rest of our lives. Rent divided by roommates multiplied by MetroCards minus food minus laundry minus, minus, minus. Factoring in the three hundred dollars I got from my insurance company after my fender bender, I figured I'd just need to get rear-ended forty-five more times to be able to live like a character on *Girls*.

This was in the Tumblr days of the internet when you could ask a person a question and they would answer it directly, usually without GIFs and political assumptions. You could get a better sense of who someone was than the foofy Instagram faux-advice of today. Shitty webcam photos led to revealing, true blog posts that were about anything and everything. Facetune hadn't become so popular that zits became obsolete on the timeline. Sharing was earnest and not a corporate buzzword to be used in place of "generating revenue." So it was no surprise that I had become fast friends with Jennifer Woods, an it-girl of the moment who had just been hired at a huge comedy show in shiny New York City. After all, a twentysomething celebrity stripped of fancy lighting and wardrobe and makeup artists is just a twentysomething, and I knew something about being one. I sent her a mixture of fan mail and general curiosity:

"Can you tell me what it was like moving to New York?" I submitted, pretending I wasn't refreshing my homepage for the moment she answered my question.

She never directly answered my question, but I remember the night I got the notification that she had followed me back, thinking, "Wow, I must be doing something right!"

She sent me a message shortly after becoming the most coveted thing you can be in these times: a mutual. I clicked so fast my off-brand laptop threatened to run its loud and ineffective fan.

"Hey! Cool hair. I'm deciding if I'm going to go natural and you've helped a ton, chica!" she wrote.

Sure, it wasn't my sense of humor, which I assumed she must have some stronger handle on than anyone else—being only twenty-two and landing such a major gig—but my hairdo that she found worthy of pressing "follow" that night. But I didn't care. So when months later she posted about looking for a roommate who wasn't an ax murderer, I thought we could totally make it happen.

I swear we're going to get back to the bus thing. Please indulge my detour.

A New York–based social media agency (that totally

doesn't exist anymore) posted an ad looking for an individual to make an entertaining video about why they should
be hired to manage other soon-to-be-nonexistent start-
ups' Facebook pages. *I was a shoo-in.* After nearly a year of
running a brand's social media pages, I learned that the one
thing it was impossible to do was inspire people to make a
video. It seemed too daunting. We had a contest once where
the rules were simple: you submit a video of you making a
cup of coffee by using a Keurig machine (which is *literally
just pressing a button*). Our newsletter had more than one
hundred thousand subscribers. Surely any of these people
could use their cell phones to take videos of them pushing
a button to win a thousand dollars, a new Keurig machine,
and box seats at an NFL game with an unlimited buffet.

Zero people even tried.

I will never know how many people took the time to
make sure they were in focus and pitch their talents to this
company, but I'm pretty sure it couldn't have been more than
five because I received an email in less than twenty-four
hours for an in-person interview a week later.

The plan was set: I'd acquire a Greyhound bus ticket,
land in Times Square with enough time to take pictures,
grab lunch with Jennifer Woods to be sure I wasn't going
to kill her and wear her skin on my face for fun, dazzle the

interviewers, and then grab dinner with a college friend before heading back home (triumphant! With a new job!) for a quick trip to pack up my stuff and finally move to New York.

My mom dropped me at the bus station around seven p.m. It immediately became clear that the lipstick I'd put on this travel pig was not gonna stick. The person behind the protective glass was less than helpful as they slid me my ticket. I had simply asked if once I got to New York there were lockers of some sort to leave my larger bag in so I wouldn't have to carry it around all day. After all, I wouldn't be staying overnight. I'd have an afternoon and then get back on the bus and come back the way we came.

"I don't work in New York."

"Oh, I know that, I'm just wondering if there's any consistency between Greyhound stations, amenities-wise?"

"What's an amenity?"

And it was settled. I'd just have to figure it out on my own.

The people who were boarding the bus seemed a little off, too. It wasn't the poverty or their cleanliness. In fact, it would appear that everyone dressed above his or her means so as to impart "I could have flown if I wanted to, but I just hate flying." No, it was the general shifty eyes and not scrolling through their cell phones to pass the time that got me. If they'd had a book, even, it would have felt like they knew they were going to be on a bus all night, and that buses are never comfortable save for when you're touring and they give you nice beds. And even then your band would be more comfortable flying from city to city, right?

I found a seat in the middle of the bus by the window. I'd read somewhere that the safest place to be on a plane if it crashed was in the cockpit or above the wing. Sans wings, the middle of the bus seemed like solid placement. The open seat gods blessed me with extra space to put my leg up if I felt so inclined. I put my backpack on the floor and wrapped one of the straps around my leg in a way that would make it nearly impossible to steal without kidnapping me, too. Once satisfied, I arranged my travel pillow between my head and the window so if sleep ever found me I wouldn't have to make direct contact. It was already dark, so the Americana I reasoned would be worth this mode of transportation was similarly obscured by night.

It wasn't long after we pulled out of the station that the meowing started. At first I thought it was just a baby whining, as did everyone. But then it became clear that there was a cat somewhere on the bus. Did it have a ticket? Where was it headed?

The bus driver pulled over on the highway and kicked a man off. Right there on the highway! Not even near an exit! Yes, he had smuggled a cat in his sweater. No, it was not allowed. Suddenly the shifty eyes and lack of distraction made sense: everyone was hiding something. I left my secrets and deceits at home! I knew I was forgetting something.

After that minor hitch, we were off for the night. No matter what awkward position I put my legs and knees in, the bus never submitted to me. I was taken back to high school, competing in speech and drama tournaments where we would often have to show up at two or three a.m. Had I ever slept on those bus trips to the middle of nowhere Kentucky? No. The thrill of being seated near any number of crushes or playing mafia until sunrise kept me awake. I was so much younger then.

Here I was, a weathered twenty-two-year-old, desperate for sleep that wouldn't come. No one worthy of crushing on in sight. In some Pennsylvania town around four a.m. we all had to get off the bus. This would have been fine, except we needed our tickets to be permitted to get back on the bus and mine was in some unreachable pocket. I tore through my backpack and purse and hoodie pockets. Nothing. Panicking, I found another unhelpful employee to sell me another ticket, somehow more expensive than my other one even though we'd already made it a quarter of the way to my final destination. I felt fleeced. I was so tired and so angry. Thank goodness for credit cards or I'd have also felt like I was overdrafting my bank account. This was not a good start to my new New York life.

Entering the bus now felt more like willful ignorance. This trip *sucked*. I was never going to get rest. I was signing myself up for having a pretty lousy day, but if college taught me anything, it was that the point is just to get through it. There's bureaucracy and seedy people and a lot of stuff you wish you could forget, but if you just get through it, life is waiting on the other side.

I sat down, flustered, and became increasingly so as a new passenger decided that sitting next to me was his best option. He was an older gentleman with Willie Nelson–style pigtails. I looked around the bus, mentally noting just how many additional open seats there were. In dire need of sleep, I just closed my eyes and laid my head back on my pillow.

Hours later I felt something touch my butt. I let it go on a little longer than necessary just to be certain that it wasn't my seat belt or a dream. Nope, it was definitely Willie Nelson's crusty hand. Still above the pants, thankfully, but by then, a twinge of New Yorker had already gotten into me, and

I turned and looked him dead in his face and just screamed. *Loud*. It wasn't words, just "AHHHHHHHHHH!"

The bus driver didn't slam on the breaks. He did get on the speaker and calmly ask, "Is everything okay?" and that's when I (still making eye contact with this douchebag grandpa) yelled, "No, this perv is molesting me!"

He grabbed his one bag and ran to an open seat next to the bus driver. Presumably making his case for why his hand needed to be not just touching, or resting, but *caressing* my ass while I was enjoying the first rest of this Oregon Trail–ian misadventure. Why, oh why, wouldn't our bus driver just try to ford the next river we came upon and drown us all out of our misery? And for some inexplicable reason this dude was allowed to stay on the bus, but the guy with the cat was presumably still hitchhiking back toward civilization.

At sunrise we stopped in Philadelphia. The bus driver again made us all exit the bus. I made sure I had my ticket in my hand and I never put it down, not even when I used the restroom at the icky rest stop. I did put it between my legs as I washed my hands, but that's because I still had standards.

My eyes burned in the sunlight, but I was relieved because the butt-rubber wasn't getting back on the bus. Obviously I wasn't going to risk going back to sleep. Bloodshot eyes would be my look of the day, but I had already overcome so much adversity in trying to get a job doing what I already knew how to do for no additional money.

It started to rain as we began the rush-hour crawl to the city. America sure is hideous in the rain. Maybe not at the beaches, but cities definitely don't benefit from the grays and stark white skies as they drip everywhere. The heating system had been activated on the bus. I knew this because I could hear it over my headphones, not because I ever felt any heat. Freezing, trying to make my hoodie a full-size blanket, I posted some lie about how great New York was to Facebook, trying to make anyone jealous of my horror-movie escapade.

New Jersey to New York was the shortest leg of the trip by miles, but seemingly the longest in duration. I half expected to descend the stairs of the bus a grizzled old man, bearded and wild-eyed like it was my first taste of freedom in decades. What had I done to deserve this, aside from being too broke to pay for a real trip to the city? If I could just survive one or two more hours on this hell-wagon I would make it to Oz, meet Jennifer the wonderful and powerful, get a job at wherever the fuck, and brag across Facebook.

When you take the Greyhound to New York, you don't *actually* get let out in Times Square, but at Port Authority.

It's a dark and dungeon-esque garage. Aboveground rats greet you. *There were lockers for you to store your extra bag.*

I found a bathroom and washed my face, brushed my teeth, put on makeup, gave up on my eye bags, and locked up my things. After a few wrong turns, I found Times Square.

And after just a moment of seeing those lights, I knew that no matter what, I was going to be on one of those billboards. I belonged here more than anywhere before it. The bus was now a distant memory, as I gazed up and saw a future filled with possibilities.

A person in a dirty Elmo costume asked if I'd like to take a picture with him. I didn't.

I sat on the big red staircase in the middle of it all. New York City, center of the universe. I took pictures in a circle, trying to capture everything for friends I knew would never visit.

Lunch with Jennifer was just lunch. As expected, she was just a person, nervous about her new job and new fame, looking for someone to hang out with and maybe sometimes share snacks. She was on the show that night, so she looked excellent. She was tall and had naturally long eyelashes. I had just ridden a bus all night. We were very different, but similar enough to remain friends now that we had met in real life.

The job interview was forgettable. The location was near my lunch date, so I arrived early, having nothing else to really do to pass the time. All of my experience was applicable. Spoiler alert: I didn't get the job. They simply didn't believe that I was actually going to move to the city. Apparently lots of people say they're going to move here. But after everything that I'd seen so far (the sweater cat(!!!)) I was definitely moving here. That couldn't have been for nothing. Still, it was a loss.

I met up with my college friend Bianca for Chinese food near Times Square. Shortly after we sat down, Russell Simmons's daughter and friends came in, too.

"This sort of thing happens all the time here. You hardly even notice it after a while," Bianca told me. Still, it was the most glamorous day of my life so far. High highs and low lows. At least it wasn't boring.

We took pictures in the now-closed Toys "R" Us. We giggled at police officers' very distinct Bronx accents. We spun around in the lights and the dirt and the cold and the bustling life that attracted so many regular people like me every day.

I went back to the bus station, vigilantly attending to my ticket and luggage. I got back on the bus.

I slept all the way to Cincinnati.

Eight Movies That Gave Me False Expectations About Living in New York

Dragging my two overweight suitcases up the stoop, I was eager to finally move into my first apartment in New York. My bedroom was the size of any Midwestern master bedroom's closet. The room faced an alleyway and had no air circulation. After I rolled my bags in, I decided to use the restroom. Upon flicking on the light, a few roaches scattered. *Not great.* The shower had baked-in footprints and blackish mold that may or may not have been a hazard for my lungs. The soap in the dish had a hair on it, too curly to go unnoticed, especially since none of my roommates had curly hair. The walls were so thin that I heard all of the exaggerated moans of my roommate's girlfriend during his odd-hour sex sessions. This was not what I thought New

York was. As an avid viewer of New York–based movies and shows, I can tell you we've all been sold a lemon. Here are the movies that gave me false expectations about New York:

1. *RENT*

Though I never saw the musical onstage, I was ridiculously enthralled by the cinematic adaptation in the fall of 2005. The plot is straightforward: A group of young friends are inordinately artistic and bohemian and broke in pre-'90s East Village, New York City. A bunch of the characters contract AIDS and sing about how scary dying is, but also how awesome it is to be young and really *stand* for something, man. I saw it in theaters twice and spent a paltry ten-dollar Best Buy gift card on the two-disc soundtrack set.

It turns out, though, that you actually *can't* protest having to pay rent after being given a free year in a big-ass studio apartment unless you're down with the whole "squatting" thing, which should be made clear from the jump. Sure, their apartments have holes in the ceiling (which I'm reasonably certain isn't up to any codes or regulations), and the only belongings they *do* seem to have in there are an answering machine, a variety of creative apparatuses like guitars and cameras, and a bike—but at least they have sunlight! Do you know how much an apartment that doesn't face a brick wall or a piss puddle goes for?! *So much money, omg.* My first apartment in this city cost seven hundred dollars a month and was shared with three Craigslist randos. We had no cell reception in the bedrooms and had to sit in the living room with the roaches if we wanted to call anyone. *Everything was made out of roaches!* There ain't nary a roach in *Rent*! How much could it have possibly cost in the early '90s to pay for an apartment where the toilet is in the kitchen?

Plus, nowadays any group of friends *that* diverse and talented would already have a hit reality show on Bravo and would not be worried about the cost of living in their freshly gentrified neighborhood.

2. *A Little Princess*

I am honestly too lazy to look up what this movie was actually about, but I sort of remember it being about a cute little white girl and her black friend who are orphans and hallucinate about living in India and colorful sand circles? And the white friend's dad isn't dead, he's just in a coma and she's waiting for him to wake up?? What I am certain of is that it rains a lot in that movie, but you don't ever see the flooded uneven sidewalks and city sludge that builds up everywhere because of it. New York is nothing if it isn't filthy.

3. *We're Back! A Dinosaur's Story*

Trust that museum dinosaurs remain inanimate and do not, I repeat: DO NOT spice up any of the city's major parades with song and dance.

4. *Autumn in New York*

I will probably never meet Richard Gere, and that is the great tragedy of my life.

5. *You've Got Mail*

Meeting a guy online is pretty much the worst thing you could do. Trust me, or at least trust my experience. A few months after moving to New York, I found a guy on Ok-Cupid who seemed totally normal and likable. We met up at a bar with his friends, who also seemed totally normal and likable. Everything was peaches and cornflakes until he suggested we go to a warehouse party in Bushwick, where he promptly decided to go snort all of the coke and ask me for sexual favors. I hopped in the first car that resembled a cab and proceeded to delete the app, my profile, and his number. Somehow he found me on Facebook and messaged me the full next day, begging for me to "pls send $20 for Chinese food xx." Ugh, *next*!

6. *When Harry Met Sally*

Maybe I'm a cynic, but if a guy repeatedly says he's not interested in you and spends decade after decade with woman after woman, maybe it's best not to wait for him to become a good guy when you're both fifty. Sure, his speech listing all your precious quirks is endearing, but get a grip! There are eight million people in this city; it's unlikely that he's the best option for you. Hell, *he* doesn't even think that he is.

7. *Breakfast at Tiffany's*

This movie is actually almost entirely accurate: parties with strange characters, a landlord who is obviously a white guy pretending to be another race very poorly, and rogue, nameless cats. I'm just really nervous about getting on the fire escape, and nobody appreciates when you sing out loud. Literally nobody. Someone should make a mash-up of Audrey Hepburn singing "Moon River" and that off-screen voice in *Coming to America* screaming "fuck you!" at Eddie Murphy.

8. *West Side Story*

Sorry, chica. That hot dude from the club doesn't search your borough for you, screaming your first name under the cover of night. He just goes home with some other hot girl he finds on Hinge, or Bumble, or Raya, or some other bull-shit "dating" app. Oh, and *they* live happily ever after.

My Clothes Suck

I blame growing up in the Ohio River Valley for my still-emerging sense of style. On any given inclement day in the Greater Cincinnati Area you can bear witness to families entering Walmart or any dining establishment in white socks with shower shoes. This fashion statement has no age limit. Pajama pants are considered both inner- and outerwear, and generally speaking, if there is a free T-shirt anywhere, it is definitely worth obtaining, keeping, and wearing out into the world.

But on the flip side, there's a culture that demands "dressing up" for flights, buying purses beyond affordability (to be fawned over at discount stores, chain restaurants, and company potlucks), and judging everyone's every trait as if we've never ourselves seen a mirror. *"Look at his shirt! Eww!" she said, pulling her jorts wedgie out of her butt crack.*

I lived in this environment until I was twenty-two.

So it should be no surprise, then, that when I moved to New York I dressed like absolute crap. The nicest things I owned were cardigans from New York & Company, *a company I've never seen in New York*, which prides itself on various watered-down collections of workplace apparel, and the pair of what I deemed "fashion Nikes" (but not fashion *blogger* Nikes) that I splurged a full fifty dollars on at a Shoe Carnival a month before moving.

To say my tops were not in conversation with my footwear would be reductive; my outfits were tragedies in three parts.

What's worse than having no personal sense of style is having good taste in spite of it. I know what looks good on my body. No matter what fluctuations or unexpected thigh-meat situation occurs, I know how to flaunt the best parts while David Blaine–ing away all of the less wonderful parts. What I didn't have was an aesthetic that I ascribed to, and thus my clothes never seemed to portray who I truly was. Game recognize game, but it's no bueno when everyone else is a giant, novel game of chess in a rose-filled courtyard and I'm a knock-off version of Candy Crush on an iPhone 2 with the sentience to understand why an iPhone X is better.

Admitting is the first step, but they should be more specific about who needs to admit to whom. I didn't necessarily need friends and coworkers chiming in on my humble aesthetic in the big city, but that didn't stop the director's commentary on my ensembles.

"Crocs are still Crocs, it doesn't matter if that pair doesn't *say* Crocs on them," Angela, the woman training me at my first big city job, warned me. She was tall in a pair of black leather sandals (with straps), a simple black blazer and matching shell, skinny jeans (dark), and simple, small gold jewelry as an accent. In hindsight maybe she thought she was training me for more than an administration position in a dusty workshop.

"But they're comfortable, work appropriate, and I can walk from Grand Central to Coney Island and they won't stink!" I protested, eager to have at least one article of clothing be deemed "not entirely heinous."

"They're made of rubber. Are you a firefighter?" she asked without taking her eyes off the Excel sheet.

"No."

"Is it raining?"

"It wasn't when I got off the train."

"Then they aren't appropriate for anything besides ruining everyone's day," she punctuated.

My shoes weren't just ugly; they inspired mood-improving drug commercials.

And it wasn't just my unacceptable footwear that required attention. All my clothes felt dated. They *were* dated, even though I purchased most of them within the past six months.

In New York, fashion has *seasons*, and style has a shelf life. *Sex and the City* taught me this, but it seemed too fantastical to be the reality of anyone who wasn't part of a tight-knit group of friends who miraculously never had a work commitment during two p.m. brunches on Wednesdays. What else had I mistaken for parody on that show? Were people *really* skipping lunch to buy *Vogue* magazine? Could you wear a ballet skirt outside on any day other than October 31st when you'd aged beyond puberty and be called "chic"? How did I get this all so wrong?

The "how" became immediately unimportant. What could be done to eradicate years of misunderstanding what was cheap but looked nice, and what was nice and looked cheap?

After Angela had satisfactorily trained me in the arts of email response, cataloguing projects, and the best place to get lunch, I was on my own with my new boss, Betty. Betty was a petite, sixty-five-year-old woman with cropped blonde hair and a daily uniform of short-sleeved black mocknecks, a medium-thick black belt with a tasteful silver buckle, tailored khakis, and black loafers. Her only jewelry included tiny pearl earrings, a thin chain bracelet, and a watch. She subsisted on seltzer and popcorn from Grand Central. Timeless. Elegant. Controlled. *Out of my price range*. I had the "talk" with her about three weeks into working together.

"Where did you get your loafers?" I asked, mentally double-checking that her classy, androgynous footwear were actually called "loafers."

"Oh these? I get the same pair every year from a shop on the Upper West Side." She remembered, "They used to come in an alligator leather, but they discontinued that some time ago."

Some time ago. Even the way she spoke was fancy! It all felt curated, not in a try-hard way, but as if she were selecting each word like a regular ordering seasonal appetizers at a rooftop happy hour. I felt like I had spent my life to that point speaking a different language.

"I don't really know how to dress." My confession hung in the air for a few moments, and then Betty patted my

shoulder and told me to grab my purse—which was actually
a Barnes & Noble tote bag.

Betty had lived her entire life in Manhattan. She'd
inherited her Upper East Side apartment from her mother
and had rent control since the '80s. Someone once told me
that people from New York are like feral animals. They
thrive only in cities and have their own knowledge and cool
about the city that is definitively exclusive. People from
New York don't usually realize how expensive things are
and how suburban the rest of the country can feel. Like
when I read Lena Dunham's book and she had a chapter
that was her food diary and she was eating, like, *celery foam*
and *mushroom essence*. I couldn't relate. I didn't know much
about what Betty's upbringing must have been besides rich
(she mentioned ballet training and European vacations a
few times), but I was happy to have a mentor who could get
me up to speed sartorially.

We exited the office and walked the half block to Mad-
ison Avenue to board an MTA bus. I had never taken a bus
in New York. Locating my MetroCard was a daily struggle,
but luckily the additional turnstiles in the subway gave
disgruntled passengers an escape from my ineptitude.
The bus riders unfortunate enough to be stuck behind
me became a captive audience for my panicky attempts to

shove the card in the machine the right direction and keep it moving.

Betty, ever city-cool, put her card into the bus's machine slot twice, getting us both on with no hassle. As we rode uptown she told me about all of the iconic stores. Their names all sounded to me like variations of that elderly Muppet duo that routinely heckled Kermit in the theater. *This store* had closed. *That store* moved downtown. *This one* was probably going out of business in a few years because Manhattan had really lost its influence to Brooklyn.

Arriving on Fifty-Somethingth street, we walked over to Bergdorf's (the Muppets' cousin's house, presumably) and sauntered inside. Did Betty realize that she was paying me five hundred dollars a week *before* taxes? That when I had "spending money" I meant I'd saved an extra twenty dollars one week that could go toward a grandma slice of pizza and maybe a mani sans pedi at the questionable place in my neighborhood on a Saturday?

Immediately upon entry I watched two salespeople spot us, and then look at our feet. One salesperson approached Betty and was off to the races describing the layout of the store as if it were the key to finding buried treasure. I was apparently beyond help and remained ignored in my depressing footwear.

Unsurprisingly, as we moseyed through section after section of fine silks and suede from every animal, I, without exception, chose the most expensive items as my favorite on each rack. As we walked, Betty talked about her theory of timelessness being the only goal in fashion and that the rest is just there to trip us up.

"This is the kind of store you should be shopping in. You don't have to buy much, because all of this is classic. So think of it as acquiring, not shopping," she said, as I tried desperately not to roll my eyes. It's a very romantic approach to dressing, but I'm broke, dude. Get real.

Weeks later, by complete accident, I attended the final "Fashion's Night Out," an event started by the fashion industry after the economy tanked due to the 9/11 terror attacks. This pregame for fall fashion week was an effort to get locals out and shopping at every store, enticed by the promise of sales, photo ops, and free snacks. My office was amid the hubbub, so walking to schmancy stores wasn't adding many steps to my day. From a distance I watched Kim Kardashian sign bottles of some fragrance she was hawking (I was absolutely not about to pay sixty dollars to smell like a magazine subscription just to get face time with Kim K.), and I saw Kristi Yamaguchi conversing with the winner of some fashion reality show. I hopped from store to store down Fifth Avenue on a humid September evening watching bloggers and hopefuls pose, desperate to be featured in street-style roundups the next morning. I realized my fashion dreams were not so deep.

My style has evolved every year of my life, and there are still days when you will catch me wearing gym clothes with no intention of setting foot inside nary a locker nor weight room. Still, I think I figured it out. Here are the only fashion rules that I try to care about:

1. Wear things that flatter your skin tone. For me and my melanin, that means the richest royal blues, ruby reds, pastels, mustards, and of course . . .

2. Black. Black is always right. Black always looks good. Do that.

3. Clothes should work in tandem with natural assets. Ruffles are dead to me. My 'fro shouldn't have to compete with '70s Elton ruffles.

4. Shoes have to be comfortable. They also have to be cute *or* true neutral. I have no problem

having unremarkable shoes. My problem is low ankles that get cut by cute shoes and hobbling up and down the stairs of subway stations, desperately hoping that there's enough space for me to sit for my sad sack ride back to Brooklyn. TL;DR: if no one remembers your shoes, that's still a win.

5.   Try to avoid buying anything I've seen my friends wear. I am always inspired by the people I know, but the original is always better than a copy.

I've since fallen out of touch with Betty, though if I'm being honest, I didn't have much in common with that rich old white lady to begin with. If I had to imagine, I'd suspect she's still rocking a very Warholian style of clothing, sustaining life solely on LaCroix and air-popped popcorn and yelling at some poor girl to draft an email for her. Whoever that girl is should absolutely ask her how to upgrade her wardrobe, and then probably start applying to more lucrative jobs. That's what I did, anyway.

Starstruck

My favorite question to get since I moved to New York is "Oh my god, how many celebrities have you seen?" The answer to this question is a *Mean Girls*-ian "The limit does not exist." What I love about this city is that everyone seems to be vibrating on his or her own wavelength of celebrity, and because of it you start to forget to care.

But to my discredit, I have a nasty predilection for embarrassment, and there are a handful of celebrities before whom I've humiliated myself. Here's a list:

Max Joseph (the silver fox from MTV's *Catfish*): On the set of a commercial and called him a "droll" when my brain attempted to say "dream" and "doll" at the same time.

Darby Stanchfield (the redhead from *Scandal*): Saw her on my Delta flight and tried to sip from the stirrer in my drink. Pretty sure she saw.

Cassie Ventura (singer of the mid-2000s hit "Me & U" and P. Diddy's girlfriend? I think?): We were seated next to each other on a flight to LA, and I knew too much about her time modeling for the Delia's catalogue and brought it up. Then I told her that "Me & U" was my first purchased ringtone and proceeded to overexplain that it was chosen because the opening lines are "You've been waiting so long, I'm here to ANSWER YOUR CALL," get it?

Jessica Alba: I was at a party with another YouTuber, Rosianna Halse Rojas, and requested a selfie, and when she refused to acknowledge our presence, her husband offered to take the photo for us.

Jenny Slate: Was interviewing the cast of a movie on the red carpet and asked if she thought Hollywood was a "boys' club" and she got really mad for some reason and told me that "all of her success was thanks to her personality and all of her failures were, too" and I frowned at her lack of engagement with the inquiry.

Matt McGorry: While attending a charity dinner I ran into him, and as he was looking for a seat I made him sit next to me in what we later determined was a toddler chair.

I forgot to get silverware and ate broccoli with my fingers in front of him. There was probably/definitely broccoli in my teeth, too.

A model I follow on Instagram: I couldn't remember her name, so then she thought I didn't know who she was but I totally did and it was so bad.

Hayley Hasselhoff: We met at an event where we were both speaking, and even after she told me her last name I asked her where she was from and never put it together that her father was Knight Rider.

Javier Muñoz (actor in Broadway's *Hamilton*, *In the Heights*): We were at a potluck, and while someone was making an important speech, my fork started falling off my plate and he had to catch it so as not to have it make a more cacophonous noise. The prong side of the fork, too. That I'd had *all* up in my mouth. He was way nicer about it than I would have been.

Marc Lamont Hill: A friend asked me to do a reading of her pilot at her apartment building and he walked in, which would have been fine except I thought he was my friend Desmond from improv.

Donald Glover: I met him on the street while he was carrying a ton of groceries and had his headphones in. I made him take off his headphones and told him how much

I adore everything he's ever done (yes, I used those words) and then begged for a selfie. He declined and I was like, "Okay." But I still posted about it online. Later, my friend Baze told me she was hanging out with Donald (first name only) and I spazzed and begged for an invite, and then when I arrived at the hotel party, I hugged Baze and knocked her wine glass out of her hand and then Donald and I had to work together to clean up the wine and broken glass. (Also, he apologized for turning down the selfie because he was in a bad mood earlier because a cab wouldn't pick him up and he had to walk two miles with groceries back to his hotel).

Christina Caradona (fashion blogger): Saw her while I was drunk at a Tumblr party and proceeded to tell her that I thought if my ex-boyfriend and I had babies they'd look like her.

Padma Lakshmi: I'd been invited to an event for her book and I promptly started complaining about how hard it is to write a book, but luckily she's super chill (considering how gorgeous she is) and she was like, "Omg, it was the hardest thing I've ever done. Books!" and I felt better.

Michael B. Jordan: I'm not sure if I verbally asked him to marry me or if it was in my head and now I'll never know. If you're reading this, Michael, I think it's cool your parents live with you and I think we would make a great pair.

New York

WHAT'S GREAT ABOUT IT?

Diversity, opportunity, and style.

WHAT SUCKS ABOUT IT?

It's the most expensive cesspool in which one can live.

End of My Relationship

The Brooklyn Museum is fancy. You might not know that if your frame of reference for New York museums are MoMA and the Met. But situated adjacent to the botanical gardens, the Brooklyn Museum in Prospect Heights is an imposing structure with a grand ivory staircase, fountains, and an all-glass, high-rated restaurant in front. This very restaurant was the site of a dinner that changed the course of my life forever.

Jazmine Hughes is not my little sister, even though I still tell people online that she is. In addition to being black and having the same surname, she's a wunderkind; an editor for the *New York Times Magazine*, she has by-lines all over town *and* is also beautiful and younger than me. Am I jealous? Who isn't? But this particular night she was profiling the Michelin-starred restaurant Saul for *New York Mag*, and I was her guest. Up until that night, in my New York tenure the fanciest thing I'd eaten was brunch in Williamsburg, which is basically just overpriced eggs, toast with nuts, oats, and more debris in it, and a side salad covered in oil and balsamic instead of ranch. This was going to be an *experience*.

I cannot recommend highly enough befriending someone with access to Michelin-starred restaurants that *checks Yelp* no longer exist but had high ratings from tourists and locals in their lifetime. The chef will do everything to impress you even when you come in wearing your Target best (which is all I can assume I was wearing because what other clothes did I have?).

"I'm meeting Darn's family over Thanksgiving," I nervously began. "I'm going to be in Nebraska with a white family I don't know for five days. No, he's never had a black girlfriend before."

Jazmine took a long sip of her first free cocktail that night. She wasn't stalling so much as preparing.

"Well, I've been with Steve for five years, so we've crossed that bridge, but here's what you should expect."

"Oh god," I said with a mixture of equal parts nervousness and intrigue. I took out my phone.

"This is off the record!"

"I'm not scooping you, I'm just taking notes! Damn, how bad is it?"

"Okay, we're back on."

As the first course of many was brought to the table, she began.

"The good news is the novelty will wear off after about an hour. But that first hour is crucial. They'll ask you a bunch of questions and try desperately to relate. Throw them a bone here."

"How?"

"Tell them you like Elton John or the Beatles. That'll give them the assurance that there's any common ground."

"Really?"

"Ha, no."

Two more presumably free rounds of drinks, please. We're going to be here *awhile*.

The truth is the only other time I'd met a boyfriend's parents, they were visiting Disney World (where their son and I worked) and were far less concerned with liking me than with talking to every cast member in Epcot about what their home countries were actually like. We hadn't been dating as long as they had been planning their vacation and wouldn't put this encounter on much of a pedestal. *This*, conversely, would be five days of unrelenting hangout in Omaha (white), Nebraska (whiter), with a family that was invested in familial tradition. Had I taken Darn to meet my mother in Kentucky, she likely would have picked us up at the airport, taken us to dinner, and then expected us to spend most of our time at the mall or a variety of chain restaurants' happy hours without her. Darn's family went *camping* together *every summer*. My family went on all of one vacation together when I was in high school. We didn't play Munchkin with all of the expansion decks. We played Spades once a decade and inevitably I'd renege and be banned from ruining my uncle's chances again.

This isn't to say that one of us had it better than the other. Truthfully, I like that my family eats together and then scuttles away to the far corners of the house for peaceful, independent reflection. The idea of a family that is all up in one another's business for days at a time is incredibly cinematic and romantic. It just wasn't what I was used to and appeared to take more energy than I like to spend on anything that isn't going to make me more attractive or wealthier.

Back at dinner, Jazmine and I were cracking up as the waiter brought us a sampling of charred octopus (a sea creature I respected too much/was too broke to ever attempt to digest), foie gras, and a beet salad. Zero of these ingredients had ever been on one of my grocery lists, but *when in Brooklyn*, I suppose . . .

"Honestly, we should make some sort of guide for white guys dating black girls for the first time." Jazmine's epiphany hit hard in the quiet of the dining room.

"Oh my god, this should be a YouTube video!"

And there it was. The idea was simple: instead of trying to glean something from Jazmine's experience, we'd proactively craft some basic rules for my boyfriend and his family. After all, it wasn't my first time spending time with white people, I just actually needed *these* white people to like me and make me comfortable lest I have to leave their home under the cover of night and find the closest Holiday Inn Express with an in-room microwave in which to have a turkey TV dinner alone.

"So what are you worried about?" Jazmine asked, half rhetorically. It's not like she didn't already know the myriad cultural differences that could be assumed. Still, some things bother some people more than they bother other people.

"The bonnet situation.[4] If I use the bathroom at night, I don't want them to say anything."

---

4   For those reading who may not be familiar with *the bonnet situation*, it is less Bo-Peep and more shower cap in nature. Basically, black hair is dainty and will break off if it rubs up against harsh cotton pillowcases. To keep curls intact and frizz-free, a satin bonnet is donned at night. It absolutely *will* slip off, causing you to wake up, blindly locate it, and resituate it on your head. Ritualistic in nature, it may seem exotic to those content to put their wet hair in a messy bun and pass out.

This made Jazmine laugh. It's not like we could control his family's actual reactions to me, but also what a specific fear.

"It's just that I haven't really even worn it around Darn," I pointed out.

"Wait, but what about your hair? You just let it tangle? 'Cause I know he doesn't have silk pillowcases."

True.

She continued, "Well, the video should definitely show you in your bonnet, but you know white people sleep in full Berenstain Bear hats and gowns,[5] right?"

Around this time in our laughter, dinner arrived. Scallops, skate (a fish, not a rollerblade), brick-oven chicken, and aged rib eye on the biggest and whitest plates I'd ever seen required the server to drag another small table over to accommodate the feast. We reached over each other to try all of the savory dishes.

"I guess I just don't want them to talk to me about *Twelve Years a Slave*. Actually, it's probably best if we don't talk about slavery at all. Do you think they'll talk about slavery?" I asked.

---

5   We know that the Berenstain Bears had a very classic and sophisticated wardrobe for bedtime, but we didn't *actually* believe that white people dressed like Ebenezer Scrooge on Christmas Eve, no matter how funny it is to think about.

"I don't think they're going to talk about slavery. They might talk about Shonda Rhimes."

"Oh my god, what are they gonna say about Shonda?" I panicked.

"They like Shonda, don't worry."

I was definitely tipsy by this point. "Okay okay okay, but is it worse if they are, like, self-congratulatory about our relationship? Like, 'We're good parents because our son is dating a black girl!'"

"Wait, what does he look like?"

I showed her a picture of us on my phone. Friends always want to see who you're dating. If I have any (good) dating advice, it's get a presentable picture together ASAP, or suffer scrolling through his (probably terrible) Instagram account for one where he looks clean, competent, and confident.

"Yeah," she began, illuminated by the blue light from my phone mixed with the dim candlelight, "his family should thank you for giving him a chance." Shade.

Darn once told me that his mom saw a picture of us together and told him, "I'm so proud of you, you're dating a woman."

"What does that mean?" I asked, fearing that perhaps he would be my second boyfriend to reveal he was gay after months of investment.

"Oh, just that I kinda always dated immature girls and you're, like, an actual adult woman," he said, which was funny because I was living with three roommates from Craigslist on a floor-bound mattress. Darn was also a You-Tuber, but he found success at seventeen and lived alone, in a one-bedroom apartment in Williamsburg at the height of its popularity (*Girls* was still on HBO, for context). I thought he was living the dream. He'd already transcended YouTube and was hosting a TV show on cable. A car was dispatched to take him to work every morning, where he'd sit in a makeup chair beside Alexa Chung. I didn't just love him, I envied him. Still, I believed that I was going to find that kind of success one day and we could succeed *together*.

Jazmine and I discussed the loathsome task of teaching Darn's family slang, should it come up.

"No, that's not what 'nappy' means. No, that's not what 'ratchet' means. Don't say 'ratchet,' please." The video script wrote itself.

The owner approached the table while we were laughing and seemed relaxed. Food writers have a reputation for being uptight and hard to please, and here we were with nearly cleaned plates, polishing off our drinks and smiling all the same.

* * *

The week before Thanksgiving, Darn dumped me. Harshly. I had already paid for the flight to Nebraska and it was non-refundable. One thing that's worse than being alienated by your boyfriend's family and seeking refuge at a Holiday Inn Express in Omaha, Nebraska, where you'll enjoy a turkey microwave dinner by your lonesome is *spending Thanks-giving alone in your apartment in Brooklyn, eating a turkey TV dinner knowing that your ex-boyfriend gets to be with his family and you get to be with your too-small TV and the cast of* Sesame Street *on the Macy's Parade broadcast.*

I was furious. In the heat of it, I broke into his apartment with a credit card (I knew he wouldn't be back for a few days—we'd booked our plane tickets together) and retrieved all of my belongings before stealing all of his light bulbs. He'd return from the airport at night with none of the lights in his apartment working. Was it juvenile? Yes. Was it badass? Yes.

The following weekend I met up with Tim, a mutual friend of Darn's, to shoot a video titled "Meet Your First Black Girlfriend." We shot all over Williamsburg, and it went live a couple days later. After writing a short description, I linked to the video on my blog and went to the bathroom.

When I returned to my room, the video already had

over a thousand reposts. This was virality. Within hours it had over ten thousand reposts. I called my mom.

"Mom, this is the big one."

"What, Kilah?"

"GO TO MY YOUTUBE CHANNEL!"

After a totally normal amount of time to wait for a page to load, I listened to my mom breathe as she watched my video. When it ended, she laughed.

"You're so goofy."

And that was that. My first real taste of "success."

When I walked into work the next morning at the social media agency, everyone regarded me a little differently. Sure, I wasn't the most famous person on earth, but there was something about multiple news and pop culture outlets organically picking up on the success of my video that elevated me in an office where our only real job was to beg news outlets to cover whatever our clients were doing. Suddenly the entry-level girl whose main job was deleting comments on the Princess Diana Facebook page that referred to her (accidentally or otherwise) as the Princess of Whales was a rising star in her own right. No one asked me to take the notes for the meeting that day.

By the next weekend, Tim and I were already hard at work on our next project. A scathing video called "Christmas

Cookies for Singles" in which I'd improvised a lament over my loneliness while cracking eggs into a bowl of powdered ingredients. En route to Tim's apartment, a person brushed past me to cross the street. I looked up to see Darn, looking back angrily. We didn't exchange words, but his face said it all. Not only was he, too, sad about the state of things, but he'd seen the video along with millions of other people.

That was all the resolution for the relationship that I needed. I'd had plenty of good ideas for YouTube videos, and Darn would convince me that the ideas weren't good, or that I shouldn't spend my time doing things without him. It had been six years since he found viral success on YouTube, and while I was thinking he was so great and had outgrown the platform, the truth was he had peaked. In a major way. As a teenager. He'd been projecting his own fear of failure onto my creative outlet, and I bought in. And why wouldn't I? *He* was the one with everything I thought I wanted. He *must* know better than me what I should do, right?

Wrong. So wrong. Oh my god, so wrong.

Another couple of days of editing and "Christmas Cookies for Singles" was published and it, too, went viral. Back-to-back viral videos. Maybe I had just gotten lucky, or maybe it was within me all along. All I knew was that having a boyfriend was good, but having a certifiable talent felt better. I spent the next year making videos for every major outlet—MTV, Oxygen, the *Huffington Post*, *Essence*, *Cosmo*—and collabs with John Green and other YouTubers with large followings. But I also spent that year feeling angry. Why hadn't Darn seen my potential? It was there the whole time, but he made me think it was silly or simply not enough. Now I'm removed enough to realize that I had to go through dating him to get to where I am today (yes, it's not just something Oprah would say, it's actually true). My relationship with Darn made me realize that my self-worth can never depend on how much someone else believes in me. There's nothing worse than being introduced by your significant other as a social media manager, or some other job title that completely misses the point of who you are and what you're capable of. Sure, I want to be in love, but not at the cost of what I've built. No fucking way.

Weight

I'm twenty-nine years old. It's the first time in my life I look in the mirror and I like my body. The curves are in the "right" place; I look like a woman and not a teenager. I can afford the clothing that looks good on me. I don't burden myself with buying smaller sizes now, in hopes of losing weight to look better in them. I just want to have a closet full of things that look good on me regardless of the size. I have no idea how much I weigh (due to careful avoidance of scales), and I no longer believe it has much of a bearing on my life prospects. I've got a huge scar on my stomach, cellulite on my thighs, and though some days are worse than others, I'm on the other side of it.

* * *

At twenty-six-and-a-half, I get the news that I have two giant tumors on my liver. I've been feeling sick anyway and can't exercise without being in a ton of pain. This diagnosis and the rapidity with which my health is failing means that I will spend the next few months on the couch. My fear and anxiety about becoming irrelevant during these inactive months causes me to binge eat ice-cream sandwiches every night. I take the trash out every morning to try to trick myself into thinking it's less of a problem than it is. My only life regret (and I spend a lot of time of thinking about it these days, given that my survival isn't guaranteed) is being so hard on my body. If there was cake at a birthday party, I made a big show of wanting it but not being able to bear what it would do to my stomach or arms or thighs. I should have just eaten the damn cake. I might be dead in a week, and I spent nearly every day of my life hating my body and denying myself good things. What a waste. In rebellion I gain twenty pounds of *fuck it* weight as the likelihood of dying seems more imminent than ever.

At twenty-five, I'm in the gym every single day. I have a short list of people who I think would be pissed off by my thinner frame—who would be jealous. They don't want me to succeed *and* they think they're better than me because

they're currently thinner than me. I've found the confidence in my video creation and comedy, but I still want to
apologize at every audition about my appearance and somehow let them know that if they give me the role, I will stop
eating to look good enough on-screen. Anytime I don't book
an audition, I assume that is why. Maybe that's what weight
always was to me: a preoccupation to push down my other
fears of inadequacy. After all, skinny people run art and
entertainment. What a privilege, to have your emotions and
struggles deemed worth sharing because your thighs are no
wider than your knees.

I'm seventeen the first time I make myself throw up. The
last time will be somewhere closer to twenty, but I'm not
thinking about living that long anyway. I lose thirty pounds
in a semester, and I stop going to classes. I cry every single
day. I sleep thirteen hours a day minimum. I'm clinically
depressed and going to therapy and taking anxiety medicine. Nothing helps. The disorder follows a major falling-out
with my group of friends from high school just before
starting my sophomore year of college. I feel like I have no
home base. A campus that isn't bad, but is seemingly in-
consequential in the scheme of the universe, fills me with
dread: a constant reminder that nothing matters, the least

of which, me and my dreams. I pass out in the middle of a presentation. I play it off simply as exhaustion. My eyesight completely fails while I wait in line to pick up birth control at Walmart, and I just sit on the ground waiting for it to return. I'm sick, and what's worse than feeling guilty that I got myself into this by ever shoving my fingers down my throat that first addictive time is being too ashamed to tell anyone what's happening to me. Living with a roommate who weighs ninety-two pounds soaking wet makes it easy for weight loss to go unnoticed. I've never felt more trapped and hopeless in my life.

My mother has made the decision that Lanie and I will switch to a public school for the rest of high school. Things were never great at Covington Latin. We had to do work-study to afford going there, but I was always assigned sweeping and dusting and as a consequence I had a lot of allergy problems that year. Plus the rich Catholics kept accusing me of stealing (I was the only black person) and my mom got tired of coming to the school explaining that we didn't even have a CD player so why would I be stealing CDs?

I built up the idea of going to a "real" high school and the *OC*-esque memories I was sure to make once I started there. But once again it isn't like that. Everyone knows I am younger, and I don't jump into extracurriculars right away. I do, however, start eating salads at lunch and coming home to do *Slimatics*, an '80s aerobic video workout, every night. In six months' time I lose forty pounds in a "healthy" way. Students, teachers, and my mom are all asking me how I've done it. I am finally known as *something*. Oh, Akilah? Yeah, she's the skinny girl. She didn't used to be, but now she's reached some unattainable goal. It's like a drug. Instead of only being known as the smart black girl, I am also thin for once.

It's a testament to how small my worldview was back then that I wanted this so badly. I had no idea that everyone was really just thinking about themselves, and that it's much better to be known as the funny or smart girl. That there's nothing inherently remarkable about my body being a certain size. But I was a kid, and nothing else intriguing was happening in my high school.

It's fifth grade, and I get a note sent home about my weight. Apparently the school nurse has classified me as overweight at 126 pounds at my age. My mom leaves it open on the counter, surely without thinking I will see it. I cry to myself that night after I eat an entire box of cereal. In a year where my grandmother passed away and my teacher is a piece of shit, being classified as different from the other kids feels like a personal failure. Here's another thing to worry about. Have the other kids noticed? Is that why none of the boys like me yet? Is that why I'm not "popular"? Of course not, but it's then that I decide to let the pursuit of being thin become half of my personality.

Most of my phone calls to friends at that age are about how skinny and pretty Britney Spears is. If only I looked like her (a girl on the other side of puberty with a team of people making sure she looks flawless daily), how much better life would be. And what's hard to admit is that I wasn't totally wrong. Yes, we live in a world where Britney Spears benefits from how attractive the world finds her. Every woman does. But to be so young as to not see that that was *wrong* and to be *overcome* was unfortunate.

Anxious Energy

THINGS THAT GIVE ME ANXIETY ON A REGULAR BASIS

- People owing me money and not paying me the money
- Missing good sales/deals because I'm waiting on said money
- Instagram. All of it.
- How my toenails look without polish
- Assuming everyone can see all of my pores
- Clutter
- Having to leave my house when I am broke
- Working out but not seeing results
- Random pains that are probably nothing, but are probably something, right?

- All the apps I don't use
- Low phone battery
- Forgetting to put things in my calendar
- Shoe dirt
- Backpack dirt
- Constant fear that thick eyebrows will go out of vogue
- Flies
- Tagged photos
- Feeling like the day is over
- The increased prospect of nuclear war
- All the books I haven't read
- Monthly subscriptions to anything
- How slow my computer is
- 3-D printers making guns
- Life

How to Make
a YouTube Video

Since begging to be considered a YouTuber and living long enough to see that become a controversial title, I have learned exactly what it takes for anyone, and I mean *anyone*, to make a YouTube video. I'm not saying this will help you go viral, and what does that even mean anymore? There are too many TV shows and movies and podcasts now to have a real cultural moment (unless you're *Stranger Things* or *Insecure* . . . are you *Stranger Things* or *Insecure*???), but that should be a motivating factor. What used to feel like a guaranteed hit can be completely overlooked thanks to the aLgOrItHm, so you just have to make what will make you feel happy and astonished that you finished a thing. Here are the steps to making a YouTube video:

1. Come up with a video idea. Usually this will happen over dinner or after watching a movie or TV show or listening to an album in its entirety or on repeat. The idea is the most important thing. YouTube videos are like jokes: if the premise isn't there, no one is going to get what you're doing.

2. Overthink how to shoot it. Your brain thinks you're Spielberg, but in reality even if you're paying people to help you, there's a high probability that because it's a thing for the internet, they will find it acceptable to drop out, causing you to go from "We're shooting this on $100,000 cameras with extras and stunt doubles" to "How can I *Nutty Professor*[6] this and shoot it on my iPhone before my battery dies?"

3. Write a script or at least have bullet points of what is supposed to happen or be said. You can go ahead and not do this if it's a vlog, but you'll probably end up with a boring-ass vlog wherein

---

6 *Nutty Professor*ing means playing all the parts yourself in full costume and voice changes. You really gotta commit.

you narrate more than you let the audience experience.

4. Take a nap. Ambition is your Waterloo. And while you would *like* to just hop to it, chances are the overwhelming pressure you have subconsciously put on yourself will cause you to lie supine on your sofa, staring into the middle distance until you pass out.

5. Make something and never be sure if it's good. Ever.

6. Agonize over the thumbnail image. Do you look pretty, or cool, or smart, or is this just a waste of time because the aLgOrItHm decides your fate and if you peek behind the curtain it is truly just an old guy pulling levers *pretending* to be the Wizard of Oz???

7. Post the video. Overanalyze why people are or aren't sharing your life's work. Are you destined to van Gogh the whole thing and only be celebrated after death?

8. Don't read the comments. Unless you love being unhappy, in which case, go wild.

9. Regardless of how "well" the video performs online, be prepared to be immediately asked to make something else good. It's not like movies or albums where you can put out one every two years and be considered a genius. Oh no, people haven't figured out that the internet can be hard work and will thus only give your success a shelf life of a week or less (thanks, Vine!). Get used to never sleeping AND never being considered truly valuable in our capitalist society. You *chose* this!

Good luck!

BB and Jennifer

Childhood friendships are so natural. Someone decides to play with you on the playground and then you just go from there. In the case of Tiffany and Stacy, life revealed whether they'd be around for the next act in my life. Adult friendships are so much harder and require so much more effort.

There comes a time—usually around 11:31 p.m.—in every woman's life when she will (out of habit) pick up her cell phone, complete the five to eight motions required to unlock her screen, and tap to open the Instagram app, where she will lazily scroll until she's received an email, a text, or maybe a tweet to distract her. She's stayed in for the evening because she's sick or she's tired and has things to do tomorrow and needs to waste just a few more minutes of time before retiring to bed. Habit.

And at this time (now 11:32 p.m.), she will scan and "like" but rarely comment on the photos of loose friends, enviable bloggers, and randos she's not even sure how she began following in the first place. It isn't much, but it shows that she supports whatever these people have decided was worthy of cropping and captioning.

But somewhere within all this scrolling she will be alerted to a pattern. *Jolted* out of her dazed and passive focus. Perhaps it only takes two photos, but no more than four, before she realizes that jarring, painful, gut-blowing truth:

All of her friends are hanging out without her.

They are smiling in slightly differently filtered and posed shots with more and more people she knows (not as well as this betrayer knows them), and she understands that somewhere along the way, she's made a very powerful frenemy who has made an apparently successful attempt to oust her from the group.

This is the story of BB and Jennifer.

Jennifer is my age. We met online before I moved to the city and while she was still very new to the entertainment industry. After some mutual following and fave-ing, I got to visit New York City for exactly eleven hours. Within that whirlwind day I got lunch with Jennifer at a small French bakery near her show's studio.

Unlike most first encounters of the internet kind, we fell into the rhythm of talking like old friends. Banter about croissants turned to lively discussion about false eyelashes, the confusing streets (how can two numbered streets intersect?!), and all the boys we never wanted to see again. The subtext of our lunch was assessing if I'd make a suitable roommate, but after moments we realized that living together wouldn't only make sense, it would also be fun. Jennifer had moved to New York very suddenly for a major job opportunity and had landed with a Craigslist roommate who was neither friendly nor stable, and I was planning to move in just a few months.

Well, like most things in my early twenties, our living situation wouldn't work out. I didn't live in New York yet, and I didn't have anyone who could guarantee the apartment. After a few challenging phone calls and many emails filled with expensive apartments I couldn't afford with no job yet secured, we both agreed that she should move on without me. She assured me we'd continue our friendship upon my arrival—that it would be *petty* to let something like this stand in the way of what was a blossoming friendship.

I moved to New York City in May 2012. Within a few weeks, Jennifer and I had brunch in a part of Brooklyn I hadn't yet explored. Greenpoint, which is accessible via my very own G train, was a total mystery. Google Maps is an app that is useful once mastered, but users should know that the first month of usage will lead to them walking miles in the wrong direction and standing on the wrong side of the street wishing they were dead. That day, Google Maps made sure that I was late. This was our first attempt to hop back into friendship since our roommate dreams got dashed, and a stupid phone app was trying to ruin this for me.

Now might be a good time to mention that Jennifer and I are in similar lines of work. She found herself very famous very quickly, and it was important to me for her to know that I respected her as a person, liked her as a person, and wasn't going to be the kind of person who would use her to get ahead. I am nothing if not maternal, and what I understood from PBS documentaries about old Hollywood screen stars was that it was the loneliness, not the fame, that drove so many of them mad. I am a good friend, and I needed her to know that.

Back to that day: I showed up about an hour late, sweaty with explosive acne showing through my nicest foundation and an uncool outfit. Jennifer was riding a major wave of press and publicity and was somehow even cooler than the first time I got to meet her. She is both impressive and relatable, intimidating and entrancing. I had met a lot of famous people in bizarre ways up to this point in my life, but I had never been close enough to order from the same waitress at the same table.

We ate a boozy brunch that went by quickly, but she extended an invitation to a cookout later that evening. We hugged. I made my way home; Google Maps made it easier for me this time.

Resisting my catlike tendencies to eat and then lie down for fourteen hours afterward, I gave Google Maps another chance and rode the G train to Williamsburg to meet up again. That summer was a particularly humid one, and I showed up frizzy and unglamorous to the third-floor walk-up apartment. The sun had set, and the cookout was hot dog remnants and an NBA game on TV. Jenn introduced me to her group of friends.

"This is Akilah. She does comedy, too!" she said nonchalantly. I was so used to adding a caveat about how I just moved to the city so I wasn't really writing or performing anywhere yet. An insecure tic meant to self-deprecate before those questions arose. But Jennifer didn't treat me like an outsider with a regular desk job. She treated me like I belonged in the glamorous world of one-bedroom apartment owners with Emmy Awards casually displayed on the mantelpiece.

Her friends were all writers and actors who welcomed

me enough for me to let loose and really be myself. After just a few minutes we were all making jokes about the game, the commercials, basically anything we could think of.

That's what I like to remember about Jennifer. She surrounded herself with good people who just wanted everyone to feel included. People like that are always getting invites to this and that, but you never get nervous about showing up or not being cute or interesting enough. Being there with them means that you're safe. There's no one to impress, because you're with the person everyone else wants to impress.

New York is a hard city. Everyone is busy, and it's not an excuse so much as an ailment you learn to live with like UTIs or sparse eyebrows. You do what you can to manage the situation so that it doesn't bother anyone else too much. As such, friends can maintain a level of closeness without actually seeing each other for a long time. Months would fly by between our brunches, day-drinking dates, and sleepovers—but it never felt like our friendship suffered because of it. Both of our careers were blossoming. Both of our love lives were blossoming. And we were up-to-date on all of it.

One night a couple years later, I performed a ten-minute stand-up set at a small-ish comedy show at UCB East. Ruby

Karp, a high-school freshman who had decided sometime around birth to do comedy, hosted the monthly show. Her mother is a feminist powerhouse who created one of America's largest feminist magazines. Between the two of them, they had a huge network of talented, cool people to perform stand-up and read their stories for an hour once a month.

I was new to stand-up and had done a few open mics up to that point, but was still very nervous to be alone onstage. Google Maps had started to like me more, so I arrived early and downed my free beverage in the green room while I considered faking sick and fleeing. I wasn't familiar with the other comics on the lineup, but hearing the show's host practice her bits and intros from the green room, I knew I should stay for everyone's set. That's when I met BB.

My set came and went, and soon enough BB took the stage. The truth is, I really liked BB's presence onstage. While there were some very rehearsed bits to her ten-minute set, she was wonderful at crowd work—which is the improv of stand-up. She could point to someone in the audience and ask them about their day, and then make a quick joke about it that kept everyone engaged and seemed to take the edge off remembering all of the words and pauses she had planned. I wanted to be just like that.

After we took a group photo, I told BB that she was

wonderful and we went our separate ways. We had a few friends in common, and when it became apparent that we'd probably work together one day, we did all the social media adding that one can do. At some point, I got her phone number and asked her for stand-up advice. She told me about a class at the premier comedy club in the middle of Manhattan she had taken, and I immediately paid the steep five-hundred-dollar rate and awaited the first course.

This, I learned, was my first mistake.

After signing up for the class online and paying the full amount, I didn't hear anything. There was no confirmation email. There was no good way to find a contact during normal hours because that's simply not how comedy clubs work. Panicking, thinking I had been scammed, I went to the club to get the weekly schedule for class. Tuesdays, seven p.m. Only have to take one train from work to get there.

The first class was not at the actual comedy club but in a rented room in a dingy building on the Upper West Side. This is not uncommon. Most of the training the people who make TV and movies have takes place in dark and dusty rooms with more character than charm.

The room was filled with mismatched folding chairs and about fifteen people of different ages and backgrounds. A seventeen-year-old wearing a suit sat next to a seventy-seven-year-old woman with a fanny pack. After a few brief introductions, it was clear that no one else in that class had ever done comedy, or had even thought about it very deeply.

"What's a pun?" a heavyset middle-aged black man wearing glasses from 1998 asked at full volume, interrupting the teacher in the middle of her opening spiel.

The class then devolved into chaos. An alcoholic lawyer from Jersey yelled an incorrect answer over a mousey girl who tried to get cell service in the dungeon to find an answer. This class was for beginners. Like, *real* beginners. There were a couple of dads in the class who were taking it again with the same teacher, because "it's always good to get a refresher."

After hearing their sets, it was clear that they were taking the class again because they had been doing the same jokes onstage since the early '90s, and there was no way in hell that they'd ever be making their writing into a career. Now, this isn't a critique of the people who chose to take this class. Everyone has to start somewhere. I'm just saying that I'm sure if a person who gets paid to choreograph dance routines and is currently working at a dance theater signed up for a dance course recommended by a dancer they admired, they'd be disappointed to find me there, dressed like a Missy Elliott music video, asking what ballet is and doing the cabbage patch.

The teacher immediately recognized the issue and pulled me aside at the end of the first lesson as everyone folded their chairs and made small talk out the door.

"I offer private lessons. This is for people who've never really ever performed or written comedy. I'll email you my rates," she offered as we headed out into the breezy Manhattan night.

I digested this information but texted BB to let her know how it went.

The class felt a little bogus, so we are gonna do private lessons, I began.

Right. I mean, it's a pretty basic class. It's just to give you a place once a week to go with your classmates. The class should be ten percent of the stand-up, and it's up to you to do the rest on your own, she defended. And that's true, practice makes perfect, and that's why I wanted to take the class.

The teacher is fine, it's just like there's no structure and almost everyone there is verrrrrrrrrry beginner. I pressed send.

Yeah, but it's a beginner stand-up class. And you're a beginner, right? she said condescendingly. How many shows have you done?

Maybe twenty? I texted.

Doing twenty shows/open mics is barely a drop in the bucket. So you are a beginner. And yeah, it's annoying that some people don't know what a pun is, but you're all novices, otherwise you wouldn't be taking the class, nah mean?

No, I didn't "nah mean." Because I was taking the class because she had suggested it. By no means did I think I was ready to have a stand-up special on Comedy Central or HBO or even on my own YouTube channel, but considering I had been booking shows for six months, writing comedy professionally, and racking up major views on my YouTube channel, it seemed a little reductive to assume that I needed to start with "See Spot run."

I told her I'd give the class a chance—and I did. I took the class to completion and performed in the class show. It was a disaster. No one was funny, and the two-drink minimum in a dark comedy club at noon on a Sunday certainly didn't lighten the room. Five hundred dollars later, and all I had learned was that reading a book about stand-up or attending shows was actually far more beneficial to my growth as a comedian than paying a tired woman to explain what a punch line was to bored strangers week after week.

I continued my day job at MTV and my weekly sketch videos for my channel, and auditioned and wrote for TV and online outlets while doing stand-up around town here and there. It was something I always wanted to get back into and really focus on, but due to other comedic success it had been repeatedly pushed to the margins of my life plan. BB and I rarely crossed paths those days, but never did I imagine she held animosity toward me for not raving about the garbage class.

In September, Beyoncé and Jay-Z's On the Run Tour was released on HBO. That same night, Jennifer invited me to BB's birthday dinner at the Meatball Shop. The vibe was chill and I made friends with other comedians in the city and their significant others. The conversation was light and filled with laughs. I assumed (naively) that things were fine.

After dinner, most of the couples left. BB and her then-boyfriend asked Jennifer and me if we wanted to go get drinks at another bar and keep the night going. *Life Lesson*: the answer is always no. No good has ever come after "keeping the night going." I'm sure of this.

A few blocks over and one drink later, the four of us sat in a booth at a mostly empty Irish pub.

"Beyoncé is just incredible. I am gonna watch the concert at least twice when I get home," I gushed. Jennifer sang the chorus of "XO" at full volume.

"Beyoncé isn't smart. And Jay-Z doesn't give back to the community," BB countered, suddenly cold.

"Well, I can't really speak to her intelligence, but I also feel like—why does *she* have to be smart? She's talented, she's beautiful, and as much as I'd like for her to be a perfect person, why does she have to carry that burden?" I asked, thinking it odd that at this moment in popular culture Beyoncé would be an unlovable character. After all, we were all still riding the wave of her self-titled album and Jennifer was probably one of the most outspoken Yoncé fans I'd ever met.

"Of course you feel that way," BB said. It hadn't occurred to me that BB would be jealous of my looks. BB isn't ugly, but she's a little older than me and doesn't have that look like she's conscious of what her clothes or makeup look like at all. She is a comedian, and I assumed she spent her time taking the ninetieth level of that shitty stand-up class or performing around town. Hmph.

Jennifer quickly finished her drink and called it a night. Missing my second chance to leave, I stayed there with BB, her boyfriend, and a few of her too-drunk friends who decided to join the festivities.

Sandwiched between BB and her deeply inebriated friend who was yelling inches from my face about why Beyoncé sucked, I finally snapped. I paid for my drinks and wished BB a happy birthday but said I *had* to run. What was fun had turned into a nightmare. A teeny disagreement about a woman who is more successful and impactful than any of us will ever be had turned into a war zone. I was woefully unarmed and unprepared to have to defend such a beloved fixture in pop culture and my personal life.

I lost my credit card, but I paid for my cab with another one. I went online to cancel the card and then fired up HBO-Go and *got every bit of my life* to the On the Run Tour. The cinematography, the choreography, the cameos, everything about it was perfect.

A week later I went to BB and Jennifer's first comedy show together. They had apparently been working on a live show where they'd banter between other comedians' stand-up sets. They'd made a YouTube video for the introduction. It was great. I was so happy for them. I posted photos everywhere online.

After the show, I caught up to Jennifer. I immediately asked her thoughts about the HBO concert.

"It was *amazing*! I kept forgetting Jay-Z was there, and then he'd, like, pop up from the stage or rotate out on a platform and I'd get so hype again!" she gushed. That was my girl. This is what adult friendship looks like.

"When you left BB's party, she started yelling at me about Beyoncé sucking. I honestly didn't know people hated Beyoncé . . ." I let slip.

"Don't listen to BB. She just likes to argue," Jenn said. And that was that.

One summer afternoon, nearly a year later, Jennifer asked me if I'd like to come chill with her, her boyfriend, and some other friends. It would be a low-key day of drinking and listening to music. I was free, so I hopped in an Uber and rode the ten minutes to her new apartment in my neighborhood. When I rang the doorbell, I was greeted with warmth from a bunch of mutual friends I'd made in my few short years in New York: a beautiful couple from Africa who were funny and enchanting writers and photographers, other comedy writers and bloggers who I'd met taking courses at Upright Citizens Brigade or working on work projects—and BB.

We were in the same room for four hours, and while I said hello and attempted to make small talk with BB, she gave me the cold shoulder until she finally decided to leave. Once she left I sat next to Jennifer on her sectional.

"Well, that was weird. BB hates me now, I guess?" I asked, hoping she'd be able to elaborate.

"Don't listen to BB. She's a hater," Jenn reassured. I wanted to press her on this, but it was a party. There's a time and place to talk out your relationship problems, and in the middle of a beautiful condo on one of the nicest days of the year with your favorite people is not the time or place.

As the sun set in Brooklyn, we turned on the On the Run Tour. Yep, still good as ever.

Winter rolled around and BB had a "black girl karaoke" event at one of my favorite karaoke spots in Koreatown. There were only maybe eight of us, but the picture we all shared on our Instagram feeds told the same story. *This is the young, black, female comedy scene in New York. We are inclusive. We are supportive. We are here.*

BB didn't speak to me. Not even a word. As I sang songs with everyone else in the room, she either sat silently or talked shit about the choice. "That rapper [of *Atlanta* and Grammy Award–winning album fame] sucks ass. I hate this song," followed by a long eye roll. As I sang with another girl who also started her career on YouTube, I heard BB make an off-color comment about how "internet comedy" isn't real comedy. I got tired. I was disappointed. I had a coupon for this karaoke establishment and got an hour knocked off our final fee. I charged the room to my card. Everyone gave me cash except BB.

Another spring arrived, and at 11:31 p.m. I chose Instagram as my sleep-procrastination method for the night. I saw a few brand-sponsored posts from bloggers and a few of my friends' drunken nights winding down. I scrolled and scrolled until I saw two pictures from different accounts, back-to-back, of BB and Jennifer and so many of our mutual friends. All of them, actually. In the back of the images were people that I'd never met and I'm not sure Jenn had, either.

I wish I had something poignant to say about losing friends. I wish I had some positive lesson about female friendship and how everyone is an adult and no one is petty. I wish I didn't feel personally responsible for jealousy directed at me because of my age or my appearance or how hard I've worked. More than anything I wish it didn't matter to me. I wish I were so strong and resilient and mythic that my feelings weren't hurt when people I care about choose bloodsuckers and leeches over genuine friendship. But maybe I don't.

So much of my life has been defined by the moments I was underestimated, abandoned, and had to wipe the tears and put on the big-girl smile and shine despite the bullshit. I used to think *that* was fake. I used to think that it was braver to fight and fight and fight, but what I'm learning is that all we have are our intentions and ourselves. People can do with them what they choose, but how can I feel down when I know that I have moved with nothing but love and honesty? How can the disdain of others affect me in any way if they've never given me anything in the first place?

And most important, how lucky am I to be in the company of Beyoncé on a petty asshole's list of "pretty but woefully untalented" people?

I'm no longer so small a person that I am actively waiting for the day her career tanks. She's tanking it in real time. And I don't wish bad on anyone, but I certainly hope that she learns from the way she's treated people she never thought were good enough or were going to make it. I'm making work in the same field, on the same networks. She's going to run into me for the rest of her life and live with the way she drove Jennifer and me apart. But Jennifer is an adult, too, so there's something to be said about how hard she fights to keep good people in her life.

In recent months, Jennifer and BB have done less and less work together. Word on the street is that Jennifer caught wise to the fact that BB has driven all of her friends away. She reached out to me to apologize for not being a good friend to me. I told her that now would be the perfect time to cut and run from BB since she's a pariah, but they're still working together.

I'm not sure what this story means in the scheme of my life. I think I've been so aware of my place in other

people's lives and that it's uncomfortable to have friends
and lose friends. That it's never easy, but also that being
friends with a person usually won't build your career, and
if it does, people will know, and hate it, and resent you for
it. That it's always better to make it on your own terms,
honestly. And that the Instagram picture is not always the
whole story.

Flirting at Every Age

Age 5: They can put their LEGOs on your LEGO structure. If anyone notices that you like them, you will be endlessly scandalized.

Age 10: A friend goes and tells them that you think they're cute. You get embarrassed.

Age 15: Attempting to sit in close proximity on the bus ride to any extracurricular event. Any physical touching whatsoever, including (but not limited to): touching your shoulder, touching your backpack, a hug, tricking you into putting your hand up to your face and then smashing their hand into your hand, causing you to slap yourself. All of that.

Age 20: Booty grabs, kisses, sexts, texts, that crap.

Age 25: Taking you on REAL DATES to places with CLOTH NAPKINS and APPETIZERS THAT AREN'T JUST POTATO SKINS AND MOZZARELLA STICKS. Making out in a clean room and them being so embarrassed by how their roommate grossed up the bathroom that they won't let you go in until they de-hair and de-grime it.

Age 30: TRIPS. Or at least I guess, I'm not there yet.

Age 35: Finding someone to babysit. If sans children, letting you sleep in on the weekends and making sure you're only snoozing on GOOD SHEETS.

Age 40: Ooh! Look at my 401(k). (Again, just guessing.)

Being Sick

The health-care system in America is broken. If the end of that sentence bored you, that's fair. I used to groan at the thought of talking about rising premiums, preexisting conditions, and misdiagnoses, too. Turns out, though, that when you almost die begging for a doctor to help you, these things all become SUPER fascinating.

In the spring of 2016, I got a rash. It was just about as glamorous as a rash can be. After working out on the elliptical for an hour, I was the most exhausted I've ever been. I walked the few blocks home, dropped my gym bag, took off all of my clothes, and lay naked on my bed for two hours before having the strength to take a shower. I was planning to shoot a video that evening, so between dramatizing what I thought was a cold and texting to push the shoot back

one, two, four hours, I washed my body, put on my face, and
headed to Tim's.

We shot a video about how patronizing articles about
#millennials are, and the time I usually spent afterward
watching new shows and brainstorming for our next shoot
was spent lying on his couch trying to explain just how tired
I felt.

Days later I had a full-blown rash and swollen lymph
nodes. I was on a flight to LA for the first YouTube Black
program ever, and I would be interviewing Mara Brock
Akil, one of my Sundance advisors, in front of an audience
of the most successful black YouTubers ever.

I made it through lunch, and through the interview, but
I felt terrible all day. I bought some aspirin during a break-
out session and hoped it would help. After feeling like I was
having a heart attack repeatedly, an ambulance had to come
and take me to the hospital.

It was clear that this was serious, but there was nothing
that could be done without a visit to a doctor first. I came
back to New York. I committed to figuring out what was
happening to me.

Imagine the most frustrating day of your life. This is a
day where everything is inconvenient and taking too long, is
too expensive, and is filled with miscommunications. Every
day of the following month was like that. I saw a variety of

doctors. I spoke with my friends' parents who were health professionals. My bank account was hemorrhaging. I was getting sicker and sicker, and doctors stopped wanting to give me painkillers to deal with the pain for fear of an addiction that would never come. One doctor offered me Xanax, as if I could relax my way out of whatever was causing the intense pain and fatigue.

Lying very still in the MRI machine, I heard a doctor's voice come over the speakers.

"Hold tight, we need to do some more imaging."

They'd said a lot without saying much at all. I'd had CT scans and MRIs after car accidents and chest pains. They were always the same. But this time they would have to do it again. I knew they'd found something. I couldn't be sure, but the tears believed it was cancer.

A day later I would get a phone call from a third doctor.

"Is this Akilah?"

"Yeah."

"Okay, so we have your imaging results."

I tried to sound calm on the phone, but I was pacing my living room with the phone on speaker. How bad was it? How long would I have to live? Would I lose all my hair? I tried to quiet the thoughts, but I knew bad news was coming.

Tumors. Three of them. Benign, but two are classified as "giant," all of my worries were confirmed.

"I'd recommend surgery, but it may be difficult to get someone to operate. It's a major surgery, and you're so young." He choked up. It was the catalyst for me sitting on the floor and crying for the rest of the evening. Soon I'd schedule more and more appointments.

A doctor who had taken the "completely removed" approach to bedside manner explained my predicament.

"One tumor is the size of a golf ball. The other—your pinky nail. And then there's the large, excuse me, giant one. It's classified as giant if it is larger than ten centimeters, and yours is just larger than that. Think *grapefruit*."

And with all of this knowledge, all of these expensive tests, all of the confirmations that there was, in fact, a real problem, I still couldn't find a doctor to sign off on surgery. I couldn't keep living like this. My days were short because I had to sleep to avoid the pain without prescriptions. I was basically at that point in *Groundhog Day* when Bill Murray's character is so sick of reliving the exact same day over and over again that he just drives off a cliff—but even that doesn't help.

It's difficult sleeping with IVs in your arm. My doctor swears that once the IV is in you can't feel it, but that's not true. I feel every pull, poke, and rub against them. And there are at least five of them. There's pain and confusion but then I remember where I am: I'm lying in bed in a room that's as dark as one can be when the door is open and there's a light on in the hallway. This time I remembered to bring my sleep mask and earplugs to quiet the incessant, unnatural beeps reminding anyone that the stranger on the other side of the curtain and me—we're both still alive.

* * *

My veins are small. Dainty, I guess. Every time I've ended up in the hospital (and my visits were becoming more and more frequent), I get stabbed at least five times, causing otherwise confident nurses to reevaluate their training. This time I've lost count of how many times blood has been drawn and how many times I've been given a spiel about how the fluid for the CT scan will burn through my veins and make it feel like I'm peeing myself, but I'm "probably not peeing myself."

* * *

"My head is killing me," I whined to my mother through the phone.

"Where does it hurt?"

"Kind of like there's a knife sticking through my forehead?"

"Take some aspirin and go to bed, Kilah," she said as if she were in the room hugging me rather than hundreds of miles away in Kentucky. I took the aspirin and I went to bed.

But the headache was still there when I woke up.

Until I got sick I thought sleeping solved everything. But lately it was just an interlude to more fear, a short break from being on the verge of tears. I never could fully accept that my life might never be normal again or that it might not last very long at all. I'd taken an Uber to the emergency room. If you call for an ambulance in New York you're never really sure which hospital you'll be taken to, so I found a favorite and stuck with it.

The doctors there ran through the normal questions: What's your name and birthdate? Are you allergic to anything? What's your pain level? What are your symptoms? And regardless of how I felt, they'd hook up an IV. I was very calm as I explained that I had a severe headache and also that for the past six weeks I'd been dealing with everything ranging from a rash to swollen lymph nodes to a strange electric shock sensation every time my body temperature changed even slightly, and, oh yes, I had a giant liver hemangioma that no one wanted to operate on because it's a major surgery and it was benign.

The CT scan results came back about an hour later as I lay in bed on my phone watching Snapchat stories from friends and choosing filters for my own.

"We're going to have to keep you overnight," the doctor said. "You said you had a headache?"

"Yeah, since last night," I reiterated.

"Well, we did a blood test, and a normal range for D-dimer to come back would be fifty to three hundred. Five hundred would be high. Yours was at three thousand."

"Okay?" I don't remember what test this was called or what it was used for, just that I was still alive, but this didn't sound promising.

"The CT scan showed a pulmonary embolism," he said.

He said a lot more things about the painful blood thinning shot I'd have to take and where I'd be admitted (New York has a lot of emergency rooms that aren't attached to a main hospital), but I just pretended to listen until he left my curtained area so I could call my mom and cry. To tell her how I'd just cheated death again. How things were more serious than ever. I tried to make her understand that there was a wall between me and the rest of the world, the dead and the living. I could feel my time running out. I was no longer hopeful, even when she told me to be. It'd been two months. My health had never been worse. I couldn't see the point in playing a game I was bound to lose.

The two EMTs loaded me into the back of their ambulance. I felt their sympathy and avoided making eye contact. It's difficult to look at anyone sick enough to be in a hospital, but there is something about a young person being ill that reminds us that death might be coming sooner than we planned. It's enough to make anyone uncomfortable.

Being on the other side of those stares was still alien to me. Staring out the back window of the ambulance, my wet eyes made the streetlights and headlights blur until I blinked and then repeated the process all over again before the doors opened at my overnight hospital.

It's now six a.m., and the nurses' station is roaring through the shift change. A doctor comes in and turns on a very bright light and tells me that after breakfast I'll have a sonogram of my legs to figure out where the clot originated. He doesn't turn off the light when he leaves.

A misconception I had about hospitals was that people got to sleep as much as they wanted there. That's not true. It's like a competition to see how many times a person can be woken up before they get angry. I concede my loss and turn on the TV, feeling sorry for myself.

Only a couple hours later, my friends Ashley and Isha show up to keep me company. They come bearing magazines, coloring books, laughs, hugs. The heavy doses of painkillers and camaraderie almost makes me forget that a lady is literally rubbing goo onto a piece of machinery and further rubbing that machinery up and down my naked body in front of them. She does ask me if I want them to leave the room, but this is the first time I've smiled in weeks. If the price of happiness is my bare ass being seen by people I love and respect, so be it.

Asking for visitors, or help, or company is something I still struggle to do. My friends sensed this and just told me what time they were on the way and if I could *please* tell them what room I was in that would make it a lot easier for them to get in. I was grateful. I'm still grateful. I can spend my entire life alone, fearing that I'm putting someone out by asking for them. And in those moments when I didn't know exactly if a future was a thing I needed to worry about, I needed people stronger than me to see through my bullshit and just make the quality time happen.

It's Memorial Day weekend, and the food all follows a theme: bland and patriotic. The modestly iced red, white, and blue cookies taste like communion wafers and add insult to injury.

It's counterintuitive but helpful to watch films more depressing than my own life at this point. I wince at *Black Swan*. I bawl to *Amy*—the documentary about Amy

Winehouse. She died at twenty-seven. I'm twenty-six. Of course I draw similarities where I can. But mostly I just watch to gain perspective. No matter how bad the exhaustion, or bloating, or aches get, I am still here.

The summer solstice hits the city, and what used to be my favorite time of year feels like an eternal winter. Whatever is happening with the sun and the moon and the crops—I want the opposite. All I want to do is hide in the dark, and for Mother Nature to normalize my lack of activity.

I start a GoFundMe, because even with my savings of around $10,000, the multiple CT scans, MRIs, doctor's appointments, and hospital bills drain that money quickly.

"Why did you post that?" my mom asks of my promoting the fund-raiser on Facebook. She doesn't mean to, but she's judging me. She's embarrassed that people know I can't afford treatment. I'm embarrassed, too. I cry.

"I don't know what else to do. I can't afford to keep paying for this, and I can't work a job because I pass out if I'm up for more than ten minutes at a time." I break down. The shame of being financially inadequate on top of being scared to death of having to move back home and give up on my dreams, or worse, *dying*, is too much.

But people give. They are so fucking generous. They

give and give. People I admire and have never met donate hundreds of dollars. People I admire and have met give even more. The shame falls away. I haven't held a gun to anyone's head and demanded they hand over their wallets. I just detailed the hole that I've gotten stuck in, and people responded with empathy and understanding. I still feel ashamed. Maybe it's because my mom worked so hard my whole life to help us appear less poor than we actually were, and here I am, announcing that I am now broke. You know that girl you look up to who left her hometown and is working for big companies in New York? Yeah, can you give her five bucks?

But the reality is I wouldn't have survived that time period being even more stressed about not being able to afford rent or the variety of medications doctors kept giving me in lieu of surgery.

* * *

Lyle, a friend and artistic partner, posted a picture of me on Instagram and I hate it. It isn't the fact that I look bloated and my eyes do that thing where they disappear because I'm laughing; it's the fact that I haven't looked like myself to me in months. It's the fact that I'm starting to not look like me to other people.

We all get used to our flaws. We learn to accept them, tolerate them, or at least find some good light and a flattering angle to hide them. So it was jarring to me to see all of my health problems reflected in a body I was already working on tolerating. Cheeks that look like they're winning the Olympic "chubby bunny" competition, curls I've been too tired to tend to, and clothing that fits awkwardly—somehow both too big and too small at the same time and in all the wrong places. More than disliking the way I look, I don't recognize myself.

That had become the theme of being sick. This isn't happening to me. This isn't me. Because it if it *were* me, I'd have to admit that I hated myself. That all of the horrible things this body was doing *was me doing it to me*, and rather than slaying some dragon, I was going to be cutting out a chunk of my body and hoping that all my organs could just stay chill for the duration of recovery. That's a scary thing to absorb.

I look terrible. I will still be this person even after I pay someone to stab me in the stomach and remove some lumps. Everything that I hate right now is actually happening and it's not happening in the past; I'm drowning in it right now.

People who mean well give me words of encouragement like:

"You're so young. In the long run this will seem like a tiny blip in your life's story . . ."

and

"We miss you!" shouted at varying decibels after midnight in a Snapchat from what looks like the best party ever—every time. Nothing helps. I start to realize that physical pain is less agonizing than watching everyone living out my days and theirs while trapped in a body that is giving up on me.

The only thing I regretted when I found out how bad the tumor was was dieting. I wished like hell that every birthday party I had eaten the cake, every movie I'd tried the popcorn, and every flight I took the damn pretzels, cookies, or peanuts. It was almost funny, really. I had gone from working out every day, counting calories, and comparing myself to literally every woman who passed me to realizing that regardless of if I was skinny or overweight, my ass was gonna die. I thought I *was* going to die. And I thought that I'd treated most people fairly and made amends for the things I'd gotten wrong, but mostly, I wished that I had been easier on myself.

* * *

There've been countless nights since the surgery that I thought I might be dying. From the first night, when I rang the bell for more medicine for so long that my neighbor in the recovery room hit their button for me, too, to the night I lay awake crying while my sister and mom lay in my living room, me being too ill to use the restroom by myself.

Healing was a long process. It took me a year to be able to feel strong enough to work out again. The scar is large and noticeable, but I'm not embarrassed. I would take four or five of those scars if it meant I didn't have to look forward to another period of my life being so horrible and isolating. But now that I know how bad it can get, I worry a lot about it happening again—the illness, the reluctant doctors, and the wishy-washy insurance. Every achievement is marred by the thought that at any moment I could feel very tired and it could be more than a cold. I don't know if I'm a strong enough person to overcome something so painful and absolutely incomprehensible again. I don't think I should have to be.

I've gone to the emergency room a number of times since getting out of the hospital simply because I had a sharp, phantom pain that I thought might be an embolism. It's madness, but caution feels warranted.

I don't know how to end this essay. I'd like for you to know that I'm also taking major advantage of having energy and good health. As much as this experience scared me, it also made me want to achieve as much as I can as fast as I can, because that loss of time felt like having my wallet stolen. Literally and figuratively. I will do everything I want to do the way I want to do it, because that's all there is.

Karaoke Is Cheaper
Than Therapy

Feelings, man. We all have 'em, and we all need to deal with 'em. We could go through the tedious task of googling a doctor, setting an appointment, remembering exactly which unpopular spin-off of our health insurance carrier we have, and talking to a stranger about our deepest secrets and insecurities for upwards of five hundred dollars a pop—OR we could realize that Frank Ocean and Cher have graciously and eloquently put our feelings to music that demands to be screamed at peak volume among friends in a dingy Koreatown karaoke bar at all hours of the night for $8.50 per person per hour.

Is there even a question which I prefer?

I take karaoke very seriously. I'm not in the school

of thought that dictates performers must sing every note perfectly and on beat with minimal lyrical flubs. Karaoke is all about stage presence and selling your emotions. Do you need vengeance? Are you scared to admit you're in love? Have you been thinking sexy thoughts all day but been too shy to speak them? Maybe you sound like a dying walrus, but that's not the point. Do dying walruses manage to make us believe they are in pain or sad or even kind of enjoying it? Do as they do. And there's no better place in the world to sing your heart song to a room filled with friends and acquaintances than in Koreatown, NYC.

K-town is pretty easy to ID and basically the only place worth visiting in Midtown Manhattan after seven p.m. Easily accessible from the 34th Street/Herald Square metro station, each building that lines the street is stacked floor by floor with Korean barbecue houses, eyelash extension parlors, and karaoke sanctuaries for the huddled masses.

Here's the ideal setup for a karaoke night:

- **8+ of your closest friends.** Fewer is okay, but usually in a group that small someone does all the singing, and the rest of the people just let them put in song after song until they slink out after they "go to the bathroom."

- **Alcohol.** I say the more the better, but I'm not a role model.

- **A preestablished vibe.** If you just got dumped and someone comes in singing the more upbeat part of Hall & Oates's collection, you played yourself.

- **A set list.** A vibe is important, but you should also know a few songs you might want to sing that you'd enjoy singing that aren't so long that everyone wants to skip your song or talk over it. Really captivate us. Short and effective is always better than the alternative. Yes, I have a note on my phone.

One time I went to France with Samsung to shoot a video. At the end of the week, after too many mojitos and a fireworks show on the beach, everyone was dragging their feet on what to do next. After all, we were in the south of France and the sun still hadn't gone down at nearly ten p.m.

That was when I suggested we find a karaoke bar. There *had* to be one. It was the middle of their tourist season and there's nothing tourists like more than group activities in sheisty bars. The group I went with was a little reluctant.

"I can stay for one song."

"I can't sing."

"Blah blah blah, I suck."

The protests never ended. But we followed the Google Maps instructions to a seedy Irish bar with "Don't Stop Believin'" blaring. *Perfect*.

Within one hour a member of our fifteen-person-deep crew revealed it was his birthday. Shots rained from the sky. We were all in. A group of Irish tourists were digging our vibe and fell in love with me and Sasheer Zamata.

Sasheer has a KILLER singing voice. A lot of people don't know this. So once she blew us all away with some Adele, the requests from the Irishmen started pouring in. For the final performance of the night we did one more shot and sang a duet to "I Will Always Love You."

I lost my voice. It's been a year and my voice is still not all the way back. The next morning I woke up with a hangover and flew to LA straightaway to VidCon. The longest flight of my life, with nothing but the memories of absolutely singing all of the most beautiful songs to a room of mostly strangers turned friends.

And isn't that what karaoke is about? You don't have to be good. You don't have to know the words. All you have to do is have a little love in your heart and supportive friends to sing with.

The Sundance Kid

Traveling is my favorite excuse to look like crap in public. I travel *ugly*. Eye crusts, a giant backpack that makes me look like a seabound turtle, a head wrap doing a questionable job of hiding my sloppily twisted hair, and the biggest hoodie and sweatpants I can find before I get to the airport. The likelihood of dying in a plane crash is pretty low, but it's the only thing on my mind when I take off and land, and I'll be damned if I'm uncomfortable when my life ends if I can help it.

Also, people who think it's important to look good for the sake of other passengers when you're sleeping for five hours in an uncomfortable chair are truly sociopaths. This is air travel, not friendship! A good flight is defined by how few times you're forced into a social interaction with the people who are inconsiderately coughing into the recycled air you have to breathe. A flight starts out at one hundred, and points are deducted every time someone asks you to get up for them to use the bathroom, bumps your arm on the armrest, or leans their chair into your lap.

So it was no surprise that when Lyle and I arrived at the Sundance resort, I looked like an absolute scrub. The only scheduled event for the first day was seven hours later. I could go from Ogre Fiona to Princess Fiona in that time, no problem. But as we stood at the welcome center with our bags, someone proposed we get lunch since we were so early, and oh, it's not a problem at all, we can take your bags to your "mountain home" for you!

Sundance is a big deal. It legitimizes me in this industry far more than a viral Vine ever did. Lyle and I shared eye contact that meant "Let's go make ourselves acceptable in the closest bathroom." And we started off in search of one nearby.

After taking roughly five steps, we heard a motorcycle approaching behind us on the walkway.

"This is where we die," Lyle said, deadpan, ready for the other shoe to drop on this dream trip.

We stepped into the grass as the motorcycle approached

and then slowed to a stop. Atop the vehicle was a man with an American flag bandana, a leather jacket, and reflective sunglasses. He turned to us and removed his sunglasses.

"Hey, ladies," he said so smoothly that my mouth dropped open.

It was Robert Redford. The Sundance Kid. *THE MOTHERFUCKING SUNDANCE KID.* I couldn't find words, but I instinctively reached into my pocket for my cell phone for a selfie. My fingers found all the buttons quickly, but the phone stalled, giving him plenty of time.

"I don't really do pictures."

And with that he replaced his sunglasses and rode off.

"ARE YOU KIDDING ME?!" Lyle screamed. We ran to the bathroom, still looking like we rode in an overhead compartment all the way to Utah. The words just flew from our mouths as we sloppily shook out our hair and applied a little lipstick.

"How on earth is this our lives? Why are we even allowed to be here?" I asked, fully meaning it.

The Sundance Labs are the incubator for TV shows, film, web series, and more. Run by true badass Michelle Satter, the program finds talented writers and puts them up for a week in swanky mountain mansions (a thing I didn't know existed) and gives them one-on-one training, advice, and therapy sessions with showrunners and network executives. Imagine it like this: your project—your show or movie or whatever—is your baby. Now imagine that you're a loving parent, hopeful for your baby's future, and then you *win the lottery* and now your baby has every good chance to make it in the world.

There are multiple objectives for the Labs. Perhaps unintentionally, one is to make friends with some of the coolest people on the planet. In my Lab alone there was the lead singer of the National and his talented editor wife, the director of a major Ryan Gosling film, an Oscar-winning documentarian couple, and more. All of us in the same boat, having our writing picked apart and made better by showrunners from the biggest shows in the HISTORY of television.

Obviously what most people want to get out of it is (1) just getting in. Thousands of people submit their projects with hopes of being one of ten projects chosen; and (2) face time with showrunners. And why not? Jenni Konner (*Girls*) and Rich Appel (*The Simpsons, Family Guy,* and *The Cleveland Show*) and Mara Brock Akil (*Girlfriends, Love Is* ___) telling you that you're funny and how to be funnier is a goddamn blessing. There's major validation at Sundance. The whole program was started because Robert

Redford found Hollywood to be less experimental and artistic than his ambition. For a person like me, who tends to feel slept on no matter how many different projects I get to work on, this was my biggest motivation.

But a lot of that excitement falls away. Not in a negative way, but in a way that makes you realize that getting in is just the beginning. The first day we watched scenes from iconic films and had screenwriters who have been in the industry for decades dissect each of them to a degree that made my head hurt. By the end of the day, I had to decompress and push away any additional imposter syndrome. The truth was I *was* green. Sure, I'd made hundreds of YouTube videos and racked up millions of views, but I wasn't a film school student. There was a lot I didn't know. I was also the youngest member of the program and I was afraid that it showed. Growing up, I always thought that once you were in your twenties, everyone would see you as an adult, but I think that people who are older than you will always see you as younger and less experienced. And they're not wrong. I'm not even sure it really *came up* in conversation or anything, but if I had to choose something to be anxious about while stranded on a mountain in a very white town, that seemed like the most acceptable thing to address. A weird predicament to be in when we live in a society that prioritizes female youth but also doesn't compensate it. If I could have frozen time and spent five years in writers' rooms and then come back, I would have.

My strongest memories from the Lab include the forever lesson that you have to drink half as much as you would at lower altitudes, because altitude sickness is REAL. I found myself crying unexpectedly, dehydrated constantly, and the one mixer where I had two drinks instead of one (bringing the feeling up to four drinks) I gushed a little too hard to each showrunner about how big of a fan I was. Way to go, Hughes. Looking totally chill and not at all like they made a mistake inviting you.

But mostly I remember feeling like I was so close to finally realizing a dream. Jenni Konner posted a photo with Lyle and me, captioned "flanked by the future of television," to her Instagram, and I really believed it. I still do. I realize that so much of my life is seeking validation that won't come for some reason or another, but in my twenties I've finally realized that success doesn't exist. The moment you feel successful, there ambition is, ready to belittle the achievements thus far in favor of striving for what's next.

In this career of mine I've befriended so many people who have amassed moments of major success and still feel like they could be doing "more." I have a friend who won an Academy Award for her documentary when she was just twenty-seven years old. I have friends who have written songs that millions of people know, but they feel like if they don't also sell a TV show then none of it was worth it. I haven't met Michelle and Barack Obama yet, but I would love to ask them if they ever feel like being the president and first lady of America for eight years was enough *success* or are we all doomed to confuse contentment with complacency?

The last day of the Sundance Labs, we had meetings with development heads at huge networks and streaming platforms. One such person asked Lyle and me what our dream was.

"To write and star in our own show," Lyle said, knowing the length at which we'd talked about this together in all the writing and bicoastal Skype calls leading up to us getting chosen for the program.

"Be careful what you wish for. You're going to get all of it," he told us. It's been a few years since, and I am working on writing and starring in my own projects. I'm not *there* yet. I am not king of the castle. But when I am, what's next?

Acknowledgments

This book wouldn't have been possible without the help of my sister Natasha and my mother, Marilynn, who supported my commitment to telling the truth, while also shielding me from lots of familial drama during the writing process. Thank you for that. Good lookin' out.

All of my love to my niece and nephews, Cameron, Mason, Nadia, Li'l Bo, and Nick. You give me hope for the next generation and you're so dang cute!

To my amazing editor, Casey McIntyre, I'm grateful for your patience and helpful suggestions that helped me do justice to my memories and comedy. You've created a monster, but, like, a cute one.

My agents and team at ICM, Katie Kolben, Ayala Cohen, Tina Dubois, Rory Platt, Kaitlyn Flynn, and Sarah

Kelly, thank you for taking a chance on me years ago and negotiating above your commission always. Love y'all to the moon and back.

I'd be remiss if I forgot to thank Berea College, Billy Wooten, Upright Citizens Brigade, Casey Neistat, John Green, Barack and Michelle Obama, the Sundance Labs, USC's Annenberg Lab, YouTube Black, Dodai Stewart, Brendan Kennedy, my hair braider Sonia, my local bodega, my mattress, and several good playlists on Spotify. It took a lot to get here, and you all helped immeasurably along the way.

Beyoncé, a steady character in my life for nearly two decades, I won't forget how you dropped self-titled right after I got dumped, or *Lemonade* coming out in the middle of my health crisis. You're a real one, Bey. You blew me a kiss at OTR II tour and magical things have been happening to me ever since. Thank you.

And a very special thanks to the doctors at Mount Sinai, especially Dr. Myron Schwartz, who didn't let me die in surgery in the middle of all this book writing. That would have been a real mess! Thank you for taking a black woman's pain seriously and saving my life.

And anyone who's looking for their name and not finding it, thank you so much for caring.